...Then
TED

To

Joshua & Bethany

Autographed
Especially
FOR YOU.

Ted KhDmianti

26. 06. 04.

...*Then Nothing Will Fail*

*An autobiographical account of the survival,
sometimes miraculous, of a middle class Polish family
during the Nazi occupation and later subjugation by the Soviets*

by

Ted Kazmierski

veranda press

Published by Verand Press
PO Box 276 Rose Bay NSW 2029

4th edition, 2002

NATIONAL LIBRARY OF AUSTRALIA
CATALOGUING-IN-PUBLICATION ENTRY:

Kazmierski, Ted, 1931-.
Then nothing will fail : an autobiographical account of the survival,
sometimes miraculous, of a middle class Polish family during the
Nazi occupation and later subjugation by the Soviets.

ISBN 1 876454 02 4

1. Kazmierski Family.
2. Poland – History – Occupation, 1939-1945.
I. Title.

943.8053092

Book design by András Berkes

Printed and bound by Southwood Press, Sydney

For the wonderful gifts of life and love
I dedicate this book to the memory
of my parents, Czeslaw and Klara.

I am most grateful to my good friend Richard Furniss whose
literary input made the writing of this book possible.

FOR SPEAKING ENGAGEMENTS
PLEASE CONTACT

TED KAZMIERSKI

38 Allonga Street
Currimundi Qld 4551
Phone: 07 5491 4968 Mobile: 0414 788 126
Fax: 07 5491 2492

Gdansk ⭐

⭐ Warsaw

⭐ Szamotuly
⭐ Poznan

Lublin ⭐

⭐ Katowice

⭐ Cracow

POLAND

C·O·N·T·E·N·T·S

P·R·O·L·O·G·U·E

The End Was Coming

TREMBLING I STOOD facing the tall brick chimney that dominated my father's knackery beside our home. Tears streamed from my aching eyes down my face. My short life of eight years was about to end – extinguished by the three-man firing squad lined up behind me. At the other side of the chimney, I knew, my older brother Hilary was also standing, his back to a similar firing squad. I prayed to God to help us.

The SS officer in his grim black uniform was shouting at me again, repeating in broken Polish the same questions, this time interspersed with guttural German which I did not understand.

"Wo sind die Waffen? Wo sind die fünf und fünfzig Gewehre?"

Fifty-five rifles? I knew of no such weapons hidden here at our family home. I had never seen any. The SS man waited. In my fear some muttering, escaped me, scarcely audible. But it was no answer. He stiffened and I sensed rather than saw the anger and frustration mounting inside him.

My Father, Czeslaw Kazmierski, in 1948

"Give me an answer!"

There was no answer I could give him.

He stamped, turned and stalked away, swinging his short cane, and disappeared behind the chimney. I could hear him bellowing the same questions at Hilary – but there was no reply. My fear mounted until my legs were shaking uncontrollably. Hilary and I were going to die together, and I wished, when it happened, we were side by side, not out of sight of each other.

The SS officer continued to move back and forth, repeating the questions, first to me, then to Hilary, his black jackboots thudding the earth. Only the metal skull above the peak on his cap and the red band with its swastika emblem on his left arm broke the black that covered him from head to foot so that I saw him as a devil coming from the bowels of the earth to destroy us.

Fear and hatred consumed my concentration upon him but somehow these feelings did not extend to the three Wehrmacht men in the grey-green uniforms. I realised they were just responding to the SS devil's commands.

He screamed at me again. "Where are the weapons?"

In desperation I blurted: "I know. A big rifle and a small rifle – and a small pistol. My father took them away to the war."

"*Nein! Nicht die!* The 55 rifles which are hidden here – in this place?"

I shook my head: I was crying again. "I don't know. I haven't seen any."

For a moment there was silence. A dreadful ominous pause. Then he roared an order to the soldiers: "Load the rifles... Take aim."

I could here the rattle of the rifle bolts – quick, precise, in unison. Now would come the order to fire. Now I would die. I was frozen in time, incapable of making a sound, unconscious of the tears, waiting for that awesome sound. Waiting... waiting... waiting...

My thoughts focussed... focussed once again on the five poor men from the nearby village of Otorowo I had witnessed being executed ten days ago in the Market Place at Szamotuly. My mother, with hundreds of others, had been marshalled into the Market Place and forced to watch the grim, simultaneous executions as a warning to all of what we could expect if we dared to resist our new German masters.

Those men too, had faced a brick wall but no questions were shouted at them. The ten soldiers of the Waffen SS firing squad had raised their weapons just once.

One man shouted out: *"Jeszcze Polska nie zginela!"* (Poland has not perished!) They had fired with such simultaneous precision that it sounded like single shot and my five countrymen had fallen.

I was rigid with terror, never having seen a human being die before. The stark meaningless cruelty of it had destroyed my childhood forever. There was nothing left now for this SS devil to destroy in me.

Just then I saw Herr Preus coming across the yard. Although he was wearing the dreaded black SS uniform, he had been our neighbour for many years. Herr Preus, who owned the nearby farm. Herr Preus who used to come to our home every month to exchange German books with my mother. He was German but he was our friend and surely he would sort things out.

He walked over to me and spoke softly, calmly, as if he did not want the other SS officer to hear him speak perfect Polish. "Ted, you must know where your father hides the weapons."

"No, I don't. I haven't seen him hide anything."

"But your mother tells me you know where they are."

I knew this could not be true. "May I see my mother, Herr Preus?"

His face darkened. *"Nein!"* His voice was loud, just like the other SS man. He turned away and spoke to the other in German – words which I didn't understand.

He turned back to me then and yelled, this time in Polish: "Turn around. Face the chimney. This is your last chance. If you do not tell us where the weapons are – you will be shot!"

I knew then, with a terrible certainty that Preus too was a devil, a devil from hell.

He walked away and disappeared behind the chimney and I could hear him in perfect Polish, delivering to Hilary the same threat he had delivered to me.

Trembling again, my face close to the yellow bricks, I prayed for the sound of the rifle fire behind me that would put an end to it all.

My thoughts turned to my father. How happy he must be now. Only days ago the news had reached us, first a telephone call from a friend, then next day an official telegram from Warsaw. My father had died in the battle for Kutno. I prayed I would see him soon in Heaven. I could recall his face so well and felt momentarily protected and secure in the vision of it. So much happiness we had shared with him. But I could find little comfort now in the message he had spelt out so often to Hilary and me. "Never be afraid. Believe in God and God will always protect you. If you believe in God – no harm will come to you."

I tried, but I could no longer believe that since my father was dead. He believed in God and God had not protected him. How could I expect God to protect Hilary and me from these two devils in their black uniforms?

And where was my mother? If she were in the house she must see me. So why does she not come out? But maybe she was not in the house because everything inside had been smashed and wrecked in the search for the weapons. But if she really loves me why does she not come to me, wherever she is, to say good-bye to me in these last moments.

The SS man was yelling again. "Where are the rifles? Tell me now." Then to the soldiers: "Load the rifles."

The routine was losing its meaning for me. The clicking and sliding and clamping on the rifles began to sound like thunder. I was aware of black squalling clouds gathering overhead, darkening the world around me. This I knew was the signal that the end was coming.

How different Preus was now from the man I had known. I thought of the many afternoons I had spend with him in the garret library of our home, helping to sort out books for him, sharing stories with him, a trusting, happy relationship. Here today, an evil opportunist in his black SS uniform, he showed no feeling for me as I stood before the firing squad.

Only last Christmas, ten months ago, he had arrived at our house during the heavy snow with his elegant sledge drawn by two fine horses in elaborate harness. He had seemed unusually happy as he shook hands with all the family and wished us a Merry Christmas, saying we all could look forward to the coming year!

What had sparked this happiness in Preus I wondered. Did he know the war was coming? That Poland would soon be overrun by the German Armies?

The sky continued to darken. All my life I had heard the country people say, whenever the dark clouds gathered, in the calm that preceded the storm, that somebody was dying. And the same thunderclouds had darkened the Market Place at Szamotuly in the minutes before the five men had been executed, bearing out the folklore of the people.

I was convinced now, with these dark clouds gathering about us, that Hilary and I were about to die. But I was also aware, and it gave me hope, that high above those dark clouds – there was God and there was heaven.

I wanted them to shoot me. To delay no longer. I was ready to die. Then my legs trembled again and my whole body shook uncontrollably. I had been standing there for time unending and my legs would no longer support me. If only this ordeal would come to an end.

The SS officer was yelling again and then I could hear the voice of Herr Preus, laughing with satisfaction. He came out of the house and spoke excitedly to the SS man and the soldiers and I wondered if he had found something. I could hear his jackboots approaching me. He pushed his big hand under my nose.

"Look at this!" He was holding a replica pistol which Hilary and I used to play with. "And this." He produced a replica sword and scabbard, a present from my father when he had visited the last World Exhibition. "Now I know you have weapons here." I didn't react. My legs had stopped trembling. A curious calm had come over me. I didn't care about Herr Preus, or the SS devil. About anything. All I wanted was for those three soldiers behind me to take aim and fire, to end the waiting, to send me from this cruel world into a happier one – where I would meet my father and find peace...

C·H·A·P·T·E·R 1

Our Last Happy Winter

AUTUMN IN POLAND has a special character, with the green leaves yellowing then deepening to a russet brown.

We lived on the edge of a vast forest where I loved to stroll with my father in the autumn evenings when he would relate stories about the shadowy people of the forest. I remember particularly one story – about a bandit who murdered a woman but was so stricken with remorse afterwards that he finally killed himself. At my tender age that story impressed me immensely.

Sometimes he would take me deep into the older areas of the forest and draw my attention to the many tall trees that had been split and charred by lightning. On one occasion he told me the story of a wealthy businessman who had driven a sulky into the forest for protection during a thunderstorm. The horse was struck by lightning and killed. In panic the man fled from the track and took shelter under a huge tree. A second bolt of lightning struck the tree and killed him.

"Never seek shelter under trees in a thunderstorm," my father advised me. "Find open space as far from the trees as you can get, or at least keep in the middle of a clearing or track. That done, nobody can help you further. Just pray and trust in God."

My father taught me what to observe in the forest and alerted me to its dangers and intrigues. Wild pigs were a constant menace. When they have young to defend they are especially dangerous and will attack people. Rabbits, foxes, deer, elks and stags haunted the dense dark areas always alert to their own dangers. After nightfall the forest came alive with owls, bats and other nocturnal creatures.

Whenever we listened we could hear the sound of the forest dwellers and I used to wonder, on occasions when my father got me to pray aloud with him, if the creatures could hear us.

Despite an awareness of the dangers in the forest – from gypsies, bandits and feral animals – I was never afraid on these walks. This was not because of my father's physical strength but because of an inner quality he possessed, which never allowed him to show fear. He was physically strong certainly but a reluctance to hurt or injure another prevented him from using this strength to force an issue. He was not the kind to take the least line of resistance either but was a person of intellectual persuasion and I felt secure in his company.

Every walk was a learning experience for me and, over time, I too learned something of my father's background. He was born in Inowroclaw, Poland, in 1898, at a time when Poland had been annexed by Prussia. He attended a Prussian school. The Polish language was banned but despite this continued to be spoken by the Polish people.

He would often arrive home from school, his body sore from beatings and his hands bloodied from caning – simply for being caught speaking Polish.

My Father, Czeslaw Kazmierski
in the Prussian Army, in World War I

In World War I, at the age of 17, he was conscripted into the Prussian army as a veterinary sergeant. In the Battle of Verdun he was taken prisoner by the French and had no qualms in discarding his German uniform, shortly afterwards and joining the new Polish army of General Haller, fighting for Polish independence.

After Poland had been freed from Prussian domination in 1918 he found himself fighting again against the Soviet Red Army occupying East Poland.

In November 1918, Poland regained its independence after 123 years of occupation by Prussia, Russia and Austria and the years between the wars were years of economic progress in Poland.

In 1926 my father married Klara Rybacka from a wealthy farming family. They bought the home and knackery where I was later to grow up, the second of four sons. This was located in a forest clearing one kilometre from Brodziszewo and seven kilometres from Szamotuly in the province of Poznan. My father began developing the knackery into a dry fodder processing plant for livestock.

My brother Hilary was born in 1928, I followed in 1931 my brother Waldemar in 1938 and Joachim arrived in 1943.

Ours was a happy childhood in a caring God-loving home bordered by the forest. An important person in our early childhood years was our loyal servant Szymon. He had been a servant of my mother's parents and – in the Polish rural tradition – had come with her to my father as part of her dowry.

A Muscovite, Szymon had deserted the Soviet Army in 1920 and joined the Polish army. Later he converted from the Orthodox Church to Catholic, changed to the Polish form of his surname Poplowski, and became a Polish citizen.

He was very loyal to my parents and indeed to us children. He was an inseparable part of our household and factory complex.

My parents did not have an easy start in married life. Two years after the fodder plant was established the Great Depression gripped Poland and lasted until 1931. It seemed for a while they would lose everything, but with help from friends and neighbours – in a spirit of co-operation engendered by the hard times – they survived. It was a debt my father never forgot and was to pay back many folds in the desolation of the war years.

My father developed a keen interest in St. Bernard dogs. He built six kennels initially for breeding them and later added another ten. As a result of this, interest in the breed was aroused throughout the district and gradually our canine population grew until we had 50 of these proud animals. St. Bernards are invaluable as guard dogs in the forest. Szymon would release them in three shifts between closing of the plant at five in the evening and re-opening at six in the morning. Shifts are necessary because some dogs had to be segregated from others.

We also had a lively little dachshund named Pursel, a short-haired red male – who was the friend of all, both humans and dogs, but was specifically Szymon's pet. Pursel and the St. Bernards gave us much joy and excitement in our early years.

The winter of 1938, the last happy winter I was to know in my childhood, was especially beautiful and remains etched in my memory even after 60 years.

In Poland at the end of autumn, nature lapses into a waiting state. The countryside becomes stark and forlorn. Then, usually around mid-November, the first snow falls and everything turns a glistening white. Around our home in the forest clearing, it was a time when all the tracks disappeared. It is in the forest that winter shows itself in its most magnificent garb. The snow settles on the branches and gradually weighs them down. In our part of the forest many young spruce trees had been planted, and young spruce trees in their garlands of snow look quite fantastic, creating a fairytale world particularly when the sun comes out and the snow glistens on the branches.

Were it not for the tall chimney stack towering over our factory complex, our home at this time would not be visible from the nearest main road or track. Under the weight of the snow, the tarred roofs of our buildings were bowed. On the ground the snow, more than half a metre deep, backed up to our windows and the first job for Szymon in the mornings was to clear this snow from windows, doors, gates and walkways.

Making snowmen, as we inevitably did at this time of year, was great fun. My parents always helped us in making a large one every year and all the boys enjoyed this. A kitchen pot provided the snowman's hat, a carrot his nose; small lumps of black coal his eyes, while potatoes gave him lips and ears. My mother provided colourful rags for his belt and our wonderful hardy creation would stand firm for two months and more until the thaw set in.

With Christmas drawing close, my mother would prepare all the good things for the festive season: honey bread topped with chocolate and caster sugar, and lots of gingerbread, much of which, kept in tins, would last us until Easter.

Christmas was always the highlight of our year and I am never likely to forget the Christmas of 1938. It was the last Christmas of my childhood I was to enjoy in peace and freedom.

At the beginning of Advent, four weeks before Christmas, we hung our stockings in the window with a list of the presents we wanted to receive.

Early on Christmas Eve we went out into the forest with Szymon and cut down the best small firtree we could find. This was set up in our living room and the work of decorating it began; always an exciting task. Szymon and the kitchen maid, Marie, helped us while our parents prepared the presents for the workers. It was the custom for the workers to leave early that day and each one went home with a present. Szymon and Marie stayed with us to share our Christmas dinner.

The atmosphere was magical, while we waited for the first star to appear in the night sky – which was the signal for the commencement of the meal.

The table was decorated in the traditional Polish fashion with candles burning (but the tree not yet lit). We began by standing around the table and my father would lead us in offering a prayer.

We sat then and my father made a festive speech, after which we passed around unleavened bread which we broke and shared with each other to the accompaniment of Christmas wishes.

There was, as usual, an extra chair at the table which remained empty. This was in symbolic expectation of our special guest, the baby Jesus, for whom there was 'no room at the inn'. Fish was a major part of the traditional menu.

After dinner with much eagerness my brother and I cleared the table and helped in the kitchen while our parents remained in the living room to light up the tree, bring out the presents and prepare to welcome Father Christmas into our home. The rest of us were obliged to wait outside in the kitchen with mounting excitement until we could hear the bells that told us Father Christmas was arriving. Finally my father's voice would call out: "Come on in, everybody. Father Christmas is here after a long journey."

In we would go – to a world of wonder. There was Father Christmas beside the illuminated tree in the otherwise dark room with a small branch in his right hand and my parents beside him. We broke into Christmas carols in the atmosphere of unbelievable joy. When this had finished Father Christmas departed, leaving us to unpack our presents in a childhood world that knew no cares or fears.

Sometime later the children of poorer families came knocking at our door and sang carols and other songs. They got honey cake and gingerbread and money from my father before moving on to the next homestead. Later that night Szymon would go out into the yard and harness the horses to the sledge to take all the family to Midnight Mass.

Next morning, Christmas Day, we were all expected to sleep in. For me and my brother Hilary there wasn't much chance of that. We had new toys to explore and enjoy. And that Christmas I had received my best ever Christmas present, a beautifully painted long sledge which could be drawn by two dogs. I was also allowed to select two of our St. Bernards for this task and chose two gentle ones. In my fantasy world they became my real live horses and gave me pride and pleasure throughout the short days of the winter months...

I had started school, aged seven, on 1st September 1938. There is no lengthy school holiday at Christmas in Poland, just a week break. Our next big festive day was Sylvester, or New Year's Eve. This was another happy day with good food and drink and singing and dancing at our home which was decorated with lanterns.

At dusk my father called us all out – my mother with Waldemar in her arms, Hilary and me along with Szymon and Marie, and led us to a small clearing in the forest. Just as he had done every Sylvester, as long as I could remember, with much ceremony he produced four small bullets from his pocket and loaded them into his revolver. He fired four shots, each in a different direction, a symbolic gesture, to thank God for the old year and to welcome the new... We didn't know it – but this time he was welcoming a fatal year for Poland and much of the world. It was 1939!

After the sound of the shots had died, the family came close together and clasped each other protectively as if – it seems to me in retrospect – we have some presentment that we were enacting this home-grown Sylvester ceremony for the last time...

My mother told me later that she noticed on this occasion that my father was 'different' as if he felt deep inside him forebodings of dark times to come. Szymon, as if he had sensed it too, turned to my father and said: "Boss, I have a feeling this has been our last happy year."

My mother, always a lighthearted optimistic person, had burst out laughing to dispel the gloom. "Don't worry," she cried, "everything is going to be all right. Come, let's go in now. It's freezing out here." And indeed it was, minus some 20 degrees centigrade.

A few hours later our first guests began to arrive and soon everybody was in a joyful mood and greetings of 'Happy New Year' rang out repeatedly until long past midnight.

C·H·A·P·T·E·R 2

A Taboo Subject

THE WHITE WINTER gradually wilted in the face of the spring thaw and the snow, dissolving, to water, flooded rivers and streams. Spring brought a new freshness full of colour. It blared its arrival in the forest around us with a profusion of lilies of the valley spreading a mottled carpet of green with tiny white blossoms. From the neighbouring villages, Szamotuly in particular, the people came every Sunday, some on foot, some with bicycles, some in horse-drawn carriages, some even by car, all with their picnic baskets, to enjoy the rejuvenation and new growth.

My father loved horses and, with the economy growing and his fodder plant thriving, he felt affluent enough to indulge this interest at last. He went around the countryside looking for a pair of special horses which would draw his elegant sulky and reflect his growing status. He located two finely bred animals, tall, prancing and fiery, but not yet tamed or broken in. They arrived at our place in a motorised horsebox. It backed up to the stable door and with some

THE AUTHOR, MOTHER AND BROTHER HILARY
IN BRODZISZEWO, 1936

difficulty and much sensitive coaxing, the two apprehensive animals were induced into the confines of the stable which was partitioned to provide compartments for each. During this operation we children were kept at a distance on my father's instruction, and nobody, even my father or Szymon, was able to relax until the stable door was closed and bolted.

These horses were wild and grew restive when anybody approached the stable – which was often because friends and neighbours would come in to admire them and my father took great pride in showing them. Not even Szymon, who cleaned the stables of the other horses, could approach them, but my father was determined to break them in and train them to harness. It took him two weeks of gentle endeavour to win their confidence until one day he managed to get bridles over their heads and take them out into the paddock. Here he attached long reins from which at first they shied and reared. Over the next few weeks he would 'ring' them in the paddock while Hilary and I, watching with my mother, would admire his strength and perseverance.

Finally came a day when he was able to harness them to his fine elegant sulky. It was an important day for him – indeed for all of us – as he dressed for the occasion in his polished leather boots and fashionable leather breeches and jacket. He looked all that he was as he climbed into that sulky, a well-to-do country businessman. He clicked his tongue loudly and slapped the reins on the foreboard, urging the horses forward. With his admiring family watching he drove out towards the forest, obviously proud of his regal turnout.

We went back to the house to wait for him, but I could sense that my mother was uneasy. I couldn't understand why, nor why he had so adamantly refused to let Hilary and me go with him. We had been in the house some 15 or 20 minutes, eagerly waiting for him to come back, when suddenly we heard a distant thunderous sound, growing, growing, and drawing closer. My mother hurried to the door and out and we heard her exclaim "Oh my God" as we ran after her. The horses were galloping at a frightening pace towards the house with manes flying. No sulky behind them! It was a second or two before I spotted my father, being dragged at a furious pace along the ground, as he clung to the reins, his body bumping over the undulations and stones.

As we gazed in alarm he suddenly let go, unable to hold on any longer. He rolled over on the earth and, slowly, painfully, climbed to his feet, torn, bleeding and dishevelled. His eyes and ours followed the horses as they changed direction and headed on towards a massive tree with a low protruding branch. They struck it together: One dead centre, sank to the ground where it stood; the other bounced off the side and over the protruding branch, fell to the ground, rolled over, kicked once and lay prone.

At this my father fell to his knees again, sickened with shock. Then he dragged himself to his feet and we could see blood on his face and hands and oozing through the shreds of his breeches and the torn ragged sleeves of his leather jacket. He heaved his huge shoulders, turned slowly, and then purposefully strode past us towards the horses without speaking. My mother held on to us, not allowing us to follow him. He stood for a moment looking down at the stricken animals, then reached down to touch them. He turned quickly and came back towards us, looking drained of all his vitality. "They're beyond help," he told my mother. "They've broken their necks. One is dead."

He went on into the house and returned with his revolver. He carried on to the horses, examined them again and put the one still breathing out of its agony while my mother took us silently inside. When he came back to the house my mother took him in her arms: he rested his head on her shoulder, saying nothing, shocked and saddened. She sat him down and while she cleaned his wounds he told us briefly what had happened.

They had trotted quietly into the woods, giving him no trouble and he was feeling satisfied with his weeks of patient work with them. He had turned them around and started on the homeward journey when a startled doe had suddenly leapt from behind the trees and darted across in front of them. Frightened, both horses had shied, then reared and bolted while he tried with all his strength to hold them. They gathered speed and suddenly the sulky wheel hit a tree stump and turned over. He had clung to the reins while the sulky was wrecked and, along with part of the shafts, was dragged behind for a kilometre or more until he could hold on no longer. One horse had died instantly on impact, its nose and forehead smashed open. The other had broken two legs. Both had broken necks.

In the weeks that followed, his fine animals destroyed, my father was so devastated he could hardly raise a smile. The wounds and their scabs were visible on his body for a long time but eventually disappeared. Not so the deep wound inside him. For him, indeed for all of us, the horses had become a taboo subject.

Months went by and with the fodder plant thriving he began to think about another business venture.

Bordering Brodziszewo was a large run-down farm which he contemplated buying, stocking and putting under a manager. He discussed this over a period with friends and business acquaintances. However, the warning signs emerging from neighbouring Germany decided him that this was not the time to embark on a new business venture.

Now, however, the word was out that he was a man of some wealth and traditionally in rural Poland, still mindful of the inflation that had followed World War I, such people tended to keep much of their assets in cash at home.

Among those who mentally noted all this was a notorious family in Otorowo. Several of the family had long criminal records and the eldest son had just recently been released from prison.

One afternoon my father received a telephone call at home and was some time on the phone before he finally put down the receiver. He was pale and clearly disturbed. He spoke quietly with my mother, ensuring that we children couldn't hear. She became visibly agitated, went to the bedroom and fetched his pistol. "Call the police, then hide somewhere and take this," she pleaded, thrusting the pistol on him. Adamantly he refused to take it.

"Too late for the police. He's coming now. I'll deal with this another way," he said.

Hilary and I grew worried, unable to understand what the drama was about. He went to the window where my mother joined him. Hilary and I followed. Shortly we saw a man in an open carriage drawn by a single horse coming along the main road and turning into our laneway.

"That's him," my father said and, turning, took Waldemar from my mother's arms, embraced him and put him down in his cot. He embraced Hilary and me in turn, then held my mother close. "Lock the door behind me when I go," he told her, "and keep the children away from the windows." He kissed her, walked to the door, stood for a moment in thought, made the Sign of the Cross and walked out. My mother, her face drawn with anxiety, locked the door behind him.

Hilary and I rushed immediately to the window but she ordered us sharply away and pointed to the couch. We knew from her tone that we had to obey her. We sat quietly and could hear our father's heavy footsteps outside fading, then the latch being raised on our metal entrance gate and the gate banging closed. After that a long silence.

We continued to sit on the couch where my mother joined us but after a while my mother could not remain still. She stood and began pacing up and down the room and gradually her agitation was transmitted to us while the expression on her face made us curious. Sensing her preoccupation, I took the opportunity to move quietly from the couch and sneak into the bedroom where another window gave me a view of the laneway. I was amazed to see my father sitting in the carriage beside the driver. His hand gestures told me he was talking very earnestly. The other was listening.

My mother came to the window beside me and was joined by Hilary: we were all safely concealed behind the lace curtain.

"Who is he?" I asked. She did not reply immediately but finally said: "I don't know." In the carriage the two men continued to talk.

After some time there was nothing left for us to do. We returned to the couch in the living room, waiting for my father to return and tell us what was happening.

The sun was sinking slowly behind the tall trees of the forest and the day was coming to an end. Half an hour must have passed and still no sign of my father returning. Then suddenly we heard the entrance gate being loudly closed and my mother sprang from the couch. We hurried with her to the window. We could see the man in the horse carriage driving down the lane towards the main road. My mother rushed to open the door and my father walked into the room. They embraced and, her face glowing, she welcomed him like the hero of Marathon. There was a faint smile on my father's face which informed us he must have had an important victory. But to Hilary and me it was no big deal he had just been up in the carriage talking to that fellow. We couldn't understand the fuss so I asked my father: "What was that all about?"

It was a couple of days before we learned the full story. He gathered us around him at the living room table and told us everything. It is a story that has remained embedded in my mind ever since.

That phone call had come from the father of the criminal family. He was an old man now, in failing health, with a feeling that he was soon to meet his Maker. He was filled with remorse for his past. His son had decided that my father was worth robbing and was now on his way to our home with a gun. The likelihood was he would kill us all. The old man had tried desperately to dissuade him, but the son wouldn't listen. He had grown up after all in an environment of crime and violence. My father should take his wife and family to safety before he got there.

My father, in a manner that I learned later in life was typical of him; decided that this was a problem from which he could not run away. Also he knew himself and realised he was not a man of violence. He doubted he could take the life of another person, even in self-defence. He made up his mind there and then to go out unarmed and confront the man. He would have to rationalise with him. That was the dangerous game he was playing in their long – drawn – out discussion in the carriage. Eventually he had prevailed, using reason and logic for persuasion. He knew when the man turned the horse to drive away, he would not have to face that trauma again.

C·H·A·P·T·E·R 3

Praying for His Intentions

O N 24 JUNE, 1939 our school year finished. I received my school report and was pleased to learn I would move to a higher class when the new school year commenced on 1 September.

I looked forward to the long summer break from school, to our family picnics, to travelling away with friends and, this year for the first time, to seeing the sea. My parents had decided they would take us to the Baltic Sea, to Gdynia, the new modern city which Poland had developed from a small fishing village after the First World War.

My parents were close friends with my schoolteacher, Mr. Rait, and his wife and they would often come with us to the meadows and the forest for our regular picnics.

The fodder plant was always busy with motor and horse-drawn vehicles moving in and out throughout the week. But my mother, who was gregarious and liked to entertain our friends, ensured that there was an equally busy flow of vehicles to our home on weekends. She was a competent pianist

OUR HOME IN THE FOREST

and our house was always a lively place with ongoing fun, card games, dancing, singing and music.

Around this time my father was travelling extensively throughout Poland and Germany on business, usually seeking new equipment for upgrading the fodder plant. Despite the threatening signs of war growing all around us, Austria, the Sudetenland and Czechoslovakia had all been annexed by Hitler's Germany, he insisted on pushing on with the modernisation of the plant while his friends and business acquaintances advised strongly against it. "The Germans will confiscate it all," they would say but he refused to listen. He proceeded resolutely with his purpose to modernise quickly while repeatedly they would ask him: "What's the purpose of all this?"

They knew he had seen in his travels the concentration of heavy equipment along the German-Polish border. He had also lived twenty years of his life under Prussia and knew what to expect... But he would take only his own council despite exhortations from my mother not to proceed. It seemed out of character because my father was a thinking and purposeful man and it was a long time before we were to learn what was in his mind.

At the beginning of July my father changed his mind about taking the whole family for the three-week holiday on the Baltic. Instead he took my mother away for a week. Clearly they had to talk everything over. When they returned my mother had changed. Now she was fully supportive of his plans to modernise.

Day by day and week by week the war clouds were gathering around us. We children, who had known nothing but peace in a carefree childhood, were finding it hard to come to grips with the threat of war. But the reality was that Poland again, after twenty years of freedom, was once more under threat.

In August my father had planned another trip to Germany to purchase equipment, but this time was refused an entry visa. This merely confirmed what he was expecting. The outbreak of hostilities was not far off. The situation was very serious.

At our evening prayers before we went to bed he would ask Our Blessed Lady to save Poland from destruction. He got us all to pray that our family would survive that our friends and neighbours would survive. Finally he would pray for the intentions of all of us. This last supplication would puzzle us. What kind of intentions did he mean?

We understood about saving our country, our family and our friends, but intentions were something we didn't quite understand.

Meanwhile, he began making plans and contingency preparations for the outbreak of war, for our evacuation before the invading armies if that was the reality we had to deal with. Two wagons were got ready and two pairs of horses. He strengthened the wagons, gave them new tyres, painted them for better protection against the weather and fitted them with canvas coverings braced with steel supports. One would provide us with shelter, the other would carry our stores – food, fuel, clothing and other essential provisions.

He briefed my mother to take control of the family wagon, he briefed Szymon to take control of the other with the food and stores. He ensured that Hilary and I were in on all this briefing but not little Waldemar who was too young and might innocently reveal things if we were apprehended by the Germans.

He realised he would not be able to accompany us. He was a member of the reserve and would be drafted into the army as soon as hostilities commenced.

He was not enthusiastic about evacuating us and treated

this as a contingency measure. He knew that ultimately there was nowhere to escape out of Poland. He had had experience of the Red Army in 1920-21 and there was no way of knowing what to expect from the East.

Regretfully but deliberately he set about reducing his packs of St. Bernard's dogs, giving many away to friends and business acquaintances and retaining just twelve dogs.

The daily news, in the papers and on the radio, was concentrated on the threatening war situation and clearly my parents were worrying. We would spend the evenings with them in the summer house in the garden and Hilary and I were more interested in catching the bats that came in towards nightfall than listening to my parents experiences of the First World War with which they were trying to imbue in us an awareness of the coming reality. We weren't interested in war experiences. We simply didn't understand war. My own interest was focussed on the new school year approaching and meeting again with the boys and girls.

The first day of September arrived with a fever of activity in our house. For me it was the big wonderful day I had been looking forward to, the start of my second year of school. Like all of that summer it was a beautiful sunny day. Because of the excitement and activity nobody bothered to turn on the wireless. Hilary left half an hour before me. He had to catch the bus for his school in Szamotuly. Before Hilary left my father blessed us both for our first day at school. Later, as I was about to go, my father took me aside and told me to make the Sign of the Cross. He impressed upon me then, as he had done many times before, that I should never leave the house without making the Sign of the Cross. It is a habit that has remained with me all my life.

I made my way through the forest to school, a walk of about one and a half kilometres, eager and happy, totally unaware of what was happening in the wider world beyond the forest. There were 26 children, boys and girls, in my class and when our teacher, Mr. Rait, usually a smiling and cheerful man, greeted us in the classroom; he was strangely subdued. His personality had changed totally. He asked us to leave everything in the classroom and come out to the oval playground because he had to address the whole school. We filed out and were joined by the children from the other classes, all chatting away and exchanging experiences of the holidays.

Mr. Rait called us to gather around him by the huge oak tree that stood in the centre of the playground. This tree was more than 400 years old, its trunk almost six metres in diameter. It would often hold us in awe when we tried to comprehend its great age and all it might have seen. His wife, who also taught at the school, now stood beside him as he commenced to speak and somehow we sensed something was terribly wrong. "My dear children, today will probably prove to be the saddest, most tragic day of your young lives, a day you are never likely to forget."

"At 4.45 this morning the German armies attacked Poland all along our western border from North to South. Since six o'clock our capital, Warsaw, has been bombarded continuously."

"This, the first day of your school year, sadly has to be our last day together."

"Now we will take part in a procession to the village and there we will meet in the church with the village people to pray. Afterwards we will return here and collect all our things from the classroom. Then each of you must go immediately to your homes."

"When we shall start our classes again I cannot tell you. That now is all in the hands of God."

We went to the village church as he had directed and, after prayers, returned to the classroom to collect our things. He was standing at the door to say 'good-bye' as each of us filed past him. He shook the hand of every child, addressing each by name. When it was my turn, he took my hand and I could see the tears welling in his eyes while he tried to stem them and at this point I realized all the happy expectancy which had built up inside me over the past few weeks was suddenly gone.

I was worried. More, I was afraid. I heard him say to me, "We'll meet again, Ted, be brave. God bless you."

I made my way out, heartsick, heading for the village, the forest and my home. Walking home I had to pass through the village before I got to the forest. There was much commotion in the street, all the women standing outside their houses chattering, many of their men, obviously returned from the fields, stood with them. There was a strange unsettling atmosphere everywhere and I quickened my pace into the forest. I was conscious of a growing sense of fear.

Beyond the forest the main road to Szamotuly was jammed with traffic, heading in both directions, the first signs of panic as people tried to move from their homes, and I was delighted when I reached my home away from the developing chaos.

My parents were waiting for me, and for Hilary who arrived about an hour later. My father halted all work at the fodder plant and sent the workers home. Only Szymon and Marie, who were part of the household, remained with us. All through the day the phone kept ringing; people wanting to speak to my father. Two of these calls were from the local office of the army reserve and recruitment. All able-bodied men up to 45 were being called up immediately.

My mother had prepared his suitcase and, when the

dreaded moment came for him to go, he embraced all of us. We were crying. He tried to assure us that he would soon be back, that we should not worry that nothing would happen to him or to us. He asked my mother to continue with the evening rosary in our home or wherever we might be. We all went with him into the village where he joined with the other men, among them the headmaster, Mr. Rait, to be transported to Szamotuly. Then my mother, Hilary and I returned home with heavy hearts.

The wireless in our house was now left on continuously and we listened with growing concern to every news broadcast. It was all bad news. Without warning five German armies had attacked Poland in the North, West and South and were advancing on all fronts. From the Baltic Sea the German cruiser Schleswig Holstein blasted our coastal towns and the Westerplatte Naval Base on the Hell Peninsula.

In our yard stood the two wagons which my father had furbished for the family's evacuation. My father had instructed Szymon to load the food and supplies into one carriage and to prepare the horses. But he told my mother not to move at this time. She should take constant stock of the situation and when she felt the time was right she should make the decision to go. He would not be able to help us because he had no idea where he would be stationed.

In the evening we were sitting in our summer house in the garden, thinking about our uncertain future and wondering what we should do when we noticed in the twilight two men in a buggy approaching our house from the main road. One climbed down and the other turned the pony around and drove off. As the man came closer I could see it was my father. My heart jumped and my immediate thought was: "Thank God. It must be all over."

My happiness was short lived as I listened to my father explain to my mother that all the draftees had been sent home to collect any firearms they had, as well as any bicycles they could find, and return with these by nine o'clock in the morning. We were grateful to God that we could all be together again even if it was only for one night.

In the morning the people gathered in the local church for prayers, then my father departed again with his two guns and a bicycle. When we returned home the wireless was announcing mobilization all over the country. The German armies were advancing: the bombardment of Warsaw continued: factories, bridges, railway stations, hospitals and military installations were being destroyed.

At lunchtime I went with my mum into Szamotuly. We could see people in long queues at the town's two mills collecting sugar and flour. People were carrying as much as they could manage. Many were preparing to evacuate but my mother had decided that we would stay.

The next day she told Szymon to cut down three tall pine trees and to fasten them as camouflage to the top of our chimneystack. This, she hoped, would deceive German warplanes. On the main road we could see crowds of evacuees moving east.

I went into Brodziszewo and saw that the villagers were abandoning everything and taking the forest road eastward. On the wireless there were warnings that German planes were shooting on refugees on the roads, that people should avoid open spaces and keep to the forest. Slowly, some of the refugees changed their minds and turned to go home causing greater confusion.

My feeling at this confusion was excitement. We had our wagons ready and could go now. It spelt adventure. I could see occasional planes in the sky and was fascinated by this new type of plane. They were still a novelty and somehow not threatening.

As I listened each day to the continuous broadcasts, with their inevitable elements of propaganda, I became convinced that Germany could not possibly win this war. That it would soon be over. In my room I made a log of all the countries supporting Germany, and of those against Germany, and the list of those against was very much longer. I felt happy.

On the third day England and France declared war on Germany. Now I was sure these two powerful nations, especially France, would take over Germany from the west in a short time. I was convinced that Germany had no chance, that my father would soon be home again.

Each day I studied the world atlas and the map of Europe and traced in my mind how the other armies and air forces would advance on Germany from the west. Day after day went by and no news from my father. Instead there was only news of German advances and heavy fighting in many places.

Hitler's Germany had been planning this attack on Poland for a long time. They were well prepared and had the most modern weapons. Now we were expecting Britain and France to attack Germany and this encouraged us to intensify the resistance. But the attack on Germany did not come. The response to the *'Blitzkrieg'* was a pathetic *'Sitzkrieg'*. That was nothing less than a mockery to us.

C·H·A·P·T·E·R 4

The Saddest News

ON THE MORNING of 7 September I went into Brodzi-szewo to see a school friend Jenny. I often played in her home. This time we weren't playing for long when we heard loud noises and shouting and suddenly three German soldiers burst into the house, rifles at the ready and ordered Jenny's mother and we children out into the yard while they searched the house.

This was my first contact with German soldiers and I was not too worried; their behaviour was not bad. They made their search and went. About an hour later, when the German soldiers had gone from the village, I said 'good bye' to Jenny and her mother and hurried home. Parked in front of our house was a military car with German insignia so I concluded the searchers were at our place too. I walked slowly into the yard. I could see no Germans there or near the fodder plant. I went into the house.

My mother and Hilary were seated at the table with four Germans in uniform, two officers and two soldiers. They were sharing coffee and cakes and the Germans were obviously enjoying it. My mother introduced me to them. She spoke perfect High German and told me what was going on. I was most impressed with the uniforms of the German officers and with their cigar boxes and their cigarette packs, Juno and R6. Noticing my interest in the cigar boxes, one German officer emptied the contents of one into the other and gave me the empty box. After finishing their coffee all stood and courteously said 'good-bye'.

The two soldiers went immediately to the vehicle waiting outside. The two officers lingered a while with my mother at the door, chatting sociably, and then they too joined the soldiers in the vehicle and departed.

It was all very amicable. I was thinking the Germans, so well dressed and well behaved, could not be all that bad. But in the evening my mother warned us that the war would certainly not finish quickly, that we would have to wait a long time for news of my father and that we must be prepared for the worst, that very bad times lay ahead of us.

The next day on the wireless an announcement from the German authorities warned that all Poles had to hand in their wireless sets. A deadline of 24 hours was given. After that time anyone found in possession of a wireless would be sentenced to death. Up to the last hour we listened for good news on the wireless but none came. Our wireless was finally handed in at the council office in Szamotuly.

When we arrived back at the house it was strangely silent, devoid of outside communication. From now on we had to depend on what we could pick up from wireless sets in German houses or on the grapevine. The telephone would ring from time to time but news was scant. I turned to playing records on the gramophone and wondered if they would soon take the gramophone from us too.

On 13 September, a dark clouded day, I went with my mother in the buggy to Szamotuly and we parked in our usual spot in the Market Square. I waited in the buggy while my mother called on some friends to see if she could get any news about my father. Suddenly German soldiers arrived with loud hailers calling on everybody to gather in the Market Square... For the first time I saw soldiers in the elegant black uniforms of the SS with big revolvers in holsters on their left hips. Hundreds of people filed into the Market Square and waited curiously, wondering what this public call was about. After some time German soldiers led in five men.

From my seat in the buggy, although I was some distance away, I could see all that was happening and could hear speeches being delivered in German which I could not understand. As the speech finished I heard a voice cry out loudly in Polish: *"Jeszcze Polska nie zginela!"* (Poland has not perished!) It seemed to come from one of the five men. Then I witnessed a firing squad of some 10 German soldiers coldly execute the five men. I could see blood spreading from the five corpses lying prone on the ground.

Next, the Germans ordered the locals to load the bodies on to a cart and to pull the cart through the street of Szamotuly. As the cart was pulled forward it left a trail of blood in its wake. Then the Germans let the people disperse.

This was my first realisation of what the Germans were capable of and it shocked me. I was trembling when my mother returned to the buggy. She climbed into the seat beside me and, as we drove home I asked her why the Germans had shot those men. "To scare the rest of us," she told me quietly, then added: "They did the same yesterday in Otorowo, shot five others. Nobody knows who will be the next or when."

MY YOUNGER BROTHER WALDEMAR WITH MY MOTHER

"But how was it those Germans at our house were such nice people?" I asked her.

"Would they too be ready to shoot anybody?"

She was silent for a while then explained: "Not all Germans are as bad as those in the Market Square. There are good Germans too. But you have to remember the Germans are very regimented and generally will obey whatever orders are given to them, even the most inhuman."

Over the next few days I had nightmares about what I had witnessed in the Market Square and pondered a lot on what my mother had told me.

In the evenings we prayed for the safe return of my father and for the repose of the dead. Whenever the phone would ring – we would all rush to pick up the receiver. Maybe it was news of father. But there was never good news, just questions going back and forth. What was happening in Szamotuly? Who had been picked up by the Gestapo and killed?

On 16 December, the Germans burned down the Synagogue in Szamotuly and blew up the monument to the Polish insurgents of the 1914–1918 war. Every day shooting could be heard from the prison in Szamotuly which was heavily overcrowded.

Late in the evening of 18 September the phone rang. My mother hurried to pick it up. She listened for a while without speaking, then finally uttered just one word, 'thanks', and put down the receiver. She sat down without turning to us and started crying.

We were both puzzled: this was not like our mum. It had to be bad news about father. Our hearts sank. We didn't have the courage to interrupt her thoughts. We waited until she was ready to explain. We were right. It was the saddest news of the last terrible 18 days. "Our father is dead. He was killed in the battle for Kutno." The man who had phoned had been fighting beside him and saw him shot.

Two days later the official telegram arrived, informing us our father had died in action.

For Hilary and me that was the first mourning of our experience. We were devastated. From that moment our home was empty, devoid of any life. Then suddenly I called to mind my father's firm assurance: "If you really believe, then nothing will happen to you." This sounded hollow to me now. After all he had assured us he would come back. Now he is dead and we don't even know where his grave is. We four are still alive and he who believed the most is not any more with us. He has left us here in the forest during these terrible times.

Gradually, as we sat there reflecting, the realization came to Hilary and me that we were no longer children. We now had to fill our father's shoes. Only Waldemar, not yet two, had the privilege of remaining a child.

One week later, 25 September, my mother called Szymon early in the morning and told him to harness the horse to the buggy. She was going into Szamotuly and was taking me with her. I was always her driver now. I liked to take control with the reins in my hands. It made me feel very grown up, a man.

She had shopping to do and friends to visit and was hoping to learn a little more about how my father had died.

It was a dull, dismal day. Everywhere along the road we passed Germans in uniform. In Szamotuly I halted the horse at our usual parking place in the Market Square and my mother went away on her business while I remained in the buggy.

Some ten minutes later I noticed a detachment of German soldiers and behind them a horse-drawn wagon carrying four policemen and four SS in their black uniforms. They were moving out of the Market Square into Railway Terrace, the way we had just come. It was these black uniformed people who had been in charge of the proceedings that day of the executions and later my mother had explained their role to me.

I didn't give this detachment much thought because there were soldiers everywhere but I told my mother about them when she returned to the buggy in the afternoon. (Our parking spot in the Market Square was outside the home of friends and they would have me in for lunch and refreshments during the day, while some of the family looked after the horse and the buggy. This always broke the monotony of the waiting and was why my mother stayed so long away this day.)

We now headed home and were still about two kilometres short of the forest, at a spot where our tall chimney stack came into view, when I noticed something odd. The pine trees, which Szymon had fixed to the top of the chimney, had disappeared.

I drew my mother's attention to this but she seemed indifferent. "The wind has probably blown them down. Szymon mustn't have fastened them properly."

We drove on and shortly came to the intersection where we had to turn right towards our home. We made the turn and were suddenly confronted by two Germans soldiers. "*Halt!* Where are you going?"

My mother explained our home was just 200 metres ahead. They stood aside and waved us on without further questioning.

As we approached our gate, a wagon similar to the one I had seen behind the detachment, was standing with its two horses. A German soldier sat in the front and behind him, bowed and dejected, was a figure I recognised, an old forester from Brodziszewo. It seemed as if he were a prisoner which made me curious. Another soldier, standing in front of our gate, threw it open for us. We drove in and were shocked to see soldiers, like busy ants, moving around the entire yard and factory area, searching everywhere. As we climbed down, Szymon came over and began to unharness the horse which he led away. We stood for a moment, looking around, trying to take everything in and suddenly we were approached by two figures in black SS uniforms. I heard my mother draw a breath. The nearer of the two was Herr Preus!

My mother stepped forward, momentarily relieved, and addressed him in perfect German "Herr Preus, *bitte*, what is going on here?"

He stared at her with no sign of recognition, his expression arrogant, insolent. *"Ich kenne Sie nicht!"*

My mother was speechless. How could Preus say he did not know us, our neighbour and our friend? I drew close to her and we walked past to the house. Preus and his SS colleague walked after us.

The scene that confronted us as we entered was beyond belief. As if some fierce whirlwind had wrecked everything. The floorboards had been ripped up, the tiles had been ripped from the front of the heating furnace; furniture had been overturned, much of it broken, locked drawers had been prised open with bayonets, my father's huge desk had been turned on it side, its drawers shattered.

Hilary and Marie clutched each other in one corner, shocked and frightened. My mother began to shake. I did too. The two SS behind us burst into loud laughter. I hated them.

Preus's colleague ordered Hilary and me to follow him out of the house. Preus remained inside with my mother. In the yard the SS officer ordered six soldiers with rifles to come with us. He led us away to the chimneystack.

Hilary, he stood facing one side of the stack, me facing the other. He lined three soldiers behind each of us. I was sure our time to die had come. He began to question us about the 55 rifles.

The Threat of Death – Our Last Prayers

EXHAUSTED AND FRIGHTENED though we were after
more than two hours of questioning interspersed with threats
and abuse, Hilary and I were still unable to give the SS officer
the answers he wanted. In the end, frustrated to exaspera-
tion, he angrily dismissed the firing squads and dragged us
both back to the house.

In the living room, Preus, another SS man and two police
officers were standing over my mother. It looked as if they
had just finished questioning her.

The SS man handed her a sheet of paper and asked her to
sign it. She began to read it and I wondered with appre-
hension what might be written there. She finally looked up
and spoke to us slowly in Polish: "Children, it says here that
we have 24 hours to produce the 55 rifles which father is
supposed to have hidden here on our property. If we fail to
hand them over we shall all be shot. I have to sign this noti-
fication." With that she picked up a pen and scribbled her
signature. As she handed back the document a sob escaped

her. The man took it from her, examined the signature, then separated the original from the copy and gave the copy to her.

They left the house immediately and we could hear their regimented strides as they went across the yard. Shortly we heard an order barked in German telling the soldiers to take formation. A minute or more went by and then we heard a single shot. We hurried to the window. The detachment had begun to march away with the wagon following behind it. Then I noticed prone on the ground where the wagon had stood the body of the old forester. He had been executed.

The message they were leaving with us was clear. This was what we too could expect – tomorrow. Seeing the old man lying there in a pool of blood we broke down and began to cry. We clasped each other, then mother gathered us around her on the sofa. We were solemnly silent, knowing there was no way out for us. Tomorrow our lives would end. Mother suddenly whispered, "Waldemar", and I saw that she was shaking as she pondered on the fate of our baby brother. Then Hilary and I began to shake too, desperate for some comfort.

I so wished my father was here, I knew that if he were and reading the document that my mother had signed, he would still be reassuring us, telling us as he always did: "If you believe, if you deeply believe, no harm will come to you." But it meant nothing to me any more. He was the one who believed the most and now he was dead. For us it was all too late. We didn't have those 55 guns. We just sat there, reconciling ourselves to death.

We kept asking each other who would have contrived this story about the 55 rifles, but could find no answer. We sat for some time, trying to settle down, but soon were crying again.

Marie was cuddling Waldemar in the kitchen and Szymon was with her. They could hear our crying and didn't want to intervene. Finally Marie came in with Waldemar. Mother took him in her arms and hugged him. After a while Marie made an attempt to tidy up the havoc in the living room but my mother told her not to bother. "It makes no sense now," she said.

Marie asked if we would like something to eat or drink. We were hungry, and thirsty, but none of us had any appetite. The living room was too uncomfortable with so many things around us wrecked and broken. We all moved into the kitchen to sit with Marie and Szymon.

Szymon liked to talk at any time and never missed the opportunity to tell a story. Now, in an effort to cheer us up, he began to tell us, in his own funny way, how one of the German soldiers had been ordered to crawl into the narrow tunnel leading to the chimney and from there to climb the internal sooty ladder to the top of the chimney to see if the guns might be concealed up there where the pine trees had been suspended. It was on this exercise that the pines had been disturbed and fallen down.

It had given him much pleasure to observe this and declined to advise the German that there was a quicker and easier way up the chimney on the outside. He laughed as he recalled how the man had emerged after about an hour, his face and immaculate green uniform blackened with soot and grime. Like us, Marie and Szymon could not understand what had come over the once friendly and affable Preus who had always got on so well with his Polish neighbours while his farm had prospered. It was impossible for them to understand how such an intelligent man could have degenerated almost overnight into a symbol of evil and cruelty in a black uniform.

As the evening wore on, Marie and Szymon grew silent like the rest of us, their thoughts finally having to focus on what fate might be in store for them too. My mother told Marie it would be better for her to go to her home in the nearby village in the morning. It would be better that she did not witness what was going to happen to the family. Marie blankly refused. She insisted she would stay with us to the bitter end regardless of what it might mean for her. That matter settled, Szymon suddenly spoke up. "And where, Madam Kazmierski, do you think I should go. I have no other home. I promise you nobody shall take me away from here while I have breath in my body."

There was an old wooden clock on our windowsill that chimed out every quarter hour of every day. It began to chime shortly after Szymon had made his point and my mother's fraught nerves gave way. She went to the window, picked up the clock and stopped the chiming operations. From that moment we were conscious of an eerie silence as the segments of each hour went by.

It might have been two hours later. I could no longer stand the morose atmosphere in the house. I went for a walk into the yard outside. It was dusk and there was nothing but silence, a strange unnatural silence. And then I noticed that even the dogs were silent. They were still locked up. This was most peculiar. Szymon had never before forgotten to let the dogs out before dark. But even little Pursil who I could see dimly lying on the steps of Szymon's out-house, was silent and very subdued. He was always a lively noisy pet, who loved to frolic whenever I approached him. But this time he didn't move. I could sense that even he was brooding, conscious of the sombre mood that was gripping all of us.

I stood for a moment convinced that Pursil too was aware of the threat of death that hung over the household. I went across and patted him but he wouldn't respond. The factory doors were still wide open. Inside just about everything had been wrecked or dismantled. It didn't matter. Nothing mattered.

I wandered around aimlessly and along the perimeter fence of our property, and suddenly I froze, rooted where I stood, startled at the sound of a whispered voice, a voice I recognised and yet a voice I couldn't recognise, a voice that was no more. I was imagining it. I looked around and could see I was alone.

Then came the voice again, whispered but lucid, articulate. "Ted, Ted, it's daddy."

No, I was not imagining this. I knew the voice so well; I loved it so much. But how could it be? Did it come from the grave? My beloved father had died a week ago. I was stifled with confusion. There was nobody visible yet the voice was so clear.

I continued to stare into the darkness without moving.

The voice again: "Ted, it's your dad." And I knew it was a living voice. I knew I was not dreaming. I wanted to jump for joy but couldn't find the strength in my legs. Suddenly I felt scared. I moved closer to the high fence from which the voice seemed to come. The voice again: "Come closer, Ted."

There was a tiny hole in the fence where a knot had fallen from the timber. I thought I could see an eye looking through.

"Is it you, daddy?" But I knew it was.

"Yes, it's me, Teddy. Are the Germans still around?

"No, they're all gone, daddy."

"Are you sure? Look around."

"They're all gone, daddy."

"Open the side gate then. But do it slowly and make sure nobody hears you."

I went to the side gate, looked around me to make sure, then very gently opened it, my heartbeats quickening with excitement, and walked out. I saw this figure standing, arms stretched towards me, and even in the half-light I recognised him clearly. He bent down as I rushed towards him, hugging him.

I was crying and I didn't know why, because I never had felt so happy. And yet, even with his arms around me, there were doubts inside me. But he had honoured his promise. He had come back. And now I was ashamed that I hadn't kept on believing him. Through heaving sobs I told him: "Now I believe all you said to me, that nothing would happen to you and that you would soon be back. It doesn't matter now that tomorrow we will not be here, we can all die together."

He held me away from him. "Teddy, what do you mean?"

"Come into the house," I told him, grasping his hand, "and mummy will show you."

As we went past the kennels, the silent St. Bernards leaped to life whining with happiness and expectation. Then they began to bark and Szymon rushed out to see what had disturbed them. He halted in his tracks and stared at us.

"Oh my God! Is it really you, boss? Am I seeing my good boss again?" This loud cry from Szymon brought everybody out from the house, Hilary, my mother, Marie with Waldemar. Everybody embraced him, clinging to his arms, and suddenly at our feet little Pursil squealed. He too had come to life and rushed to my father's feet and one of us had stepped on him.

We all went into the house together and, at the sight of the living room, my father stopped, incredulous. "What's all this about?" he asked us.

By now my mother had recovered and was calm but she couldn't find the words to tell him. She picked up the copy of the document she had signed and handed it to him.

M Y YOUNGEST BROTHER JOAHIM AND THE SNOW MAN

My father read it slowly. When at the bottom he recognised the signature of Preus he was lost for words. He sat down on the upturned desk and pondered silently for a minute or two. He looked up at last and turned to my mother. "Is this the same Preus who comes to our home and borrows your books?"

"The same one," she told him, "but in a different cloak, a black SS uniform. He denied that he knew us. He insisted that we have 55 rifles hidden here on our property."

My father pondered briefly again before speaking. "Is Preus then so unfortunate a human being that he stoops so far below human dignity? May God have mercy on him."

He could not conceive what rifles they might be looking for. "This has to be the product of a deranged mind that he would murder all of us to ingratiate himself with his SS hierarchy. This is so low, so contemptible, it defies belief. Always we have treated him as a decent German and this is how he repays us." As was his character he was more deeply upset than angry. "No, no. I am sure God will not allow this evil intent to be fulfilled. Sooner or later, Preus will be punished." (We were to learn in time that in the first week of the German attack on Russia, Preus was killed on the Eastern front.)

Now my father, as I had seen him do often before, called on his great reserve of patience and settled down to think things over. He asked Marie to make some supper, remarking that he was tired and hungry. While we were eating he explained that he had survived at Kutno because he had been trapped under the corpses of a couple of his colleagues and had feigned dead until nightfall when he had escaped to the forest. For more than a week he had been making his way home, keeping mainly to the forests.

"I was hiding outside for several hours this afternoon when I saw that the Germans were searching. I retreated into the forest, but later heard a shot and saw them departing. I came close to the fence after that and waited for somebody to come out. I couldn't be sure they had all left. The fact that the dogs weren't barking, suggested to me that some Germans were still around."

We concentrated on listening to him rather than eating. I was hungry, but had no appetite and was sure the others felt the same way. When he observed he was the only one eating, he said: "What's this about? Tomorrow we have a big day in front of us. We're going to need our strength, so please, everybody, eat."

Hilary and I exchanged glances with our mother. We were all thinking alike. "A long day ahead!" Didn't he realise, it would be a short day – our shortest and our last.

Reluctantly we began to eat and gradually my father's huge appetite made the rest of us hungry too.

After supper he reminded Szymon he should let the dogs out and afterwards come back and help us tidy up the house.

"We don't need any broken limbs," he added by way of caution.

We all set to work helping to get the house back in order. First, we gathered up the furnace tiles scattered around the damaged floor area and carried them outside in a wheel-barrow. Then we righted the huge desk and the other furniture and straightened as many floorboards as we could manage. Inevitably we asked him: "Does all this make sense?" Even my mother was tidying the bedroom and it seemed to be entirely futile. He simply told us to get on with it.

The hour was now approaching our bedtime and my father asked us to kneel by the bedside to pray. It was something I was expecting, as I felt sure it was with Hilary too. Now, once again, after a lapse of some three weeks, we were saying our night prayers with our father again. We felt happy and secure and it seemed for a little that everything was, as it had always been that nothing had changed.

But it only needed a short lapse of concentration and a glance around me to see the reality that everything had changed. Then my mother began to cry and immediately Hilary cried too. These would be our last prayers together. Tomorrow our lives would end. As we got to our feet, my father repeated the same aspiration with which he had always sent us to bed. "Sleep with God, my sons." This time he added: "I want to talk to your mother for a little while, but we'll turn in soon because we're both very tired."

It was long after midnight when we heard them going to bed. Neither Hilary nor I slept a wink. We could not escape the awareness that this would be our last night. I reflected many times on the old forester and wondered if that was how they would shoot us too. But now at least we would all die together.

About six in the morning I heard my parents getting up very quietly: so quietly in fact I realised they were trying not to wake us. But Hilary and I hadn't slept. As soon as my father observed we were awake, he told us to go back to sleep that he would wake us up later. A little later I heard him moving about in the yard and I guessed he was searching for the old bicycle he had left behind when he went to the war. Then I heard the sound of him pumping the tyres.

After they had their breakfast, my parents came to the bedroom and told us they were going to see the German Wehrmacht commander in Szamotuly, not the Gestapo or the police. We didn't then understand the significance of this as we would later on. They told us to be calm, not to fear, and, as always, my father insisted we would be all right. They mounted their bicycles, leaving us with Marie and Szymon, but neither Hilary nor I could understand how he dared to approach the Germans. We climbed from our beds and dressed immediately.

Confused thoughts tormented my mind. What had come over my father? He had escaped death in battle; he had avoided being taken prisoner, and now on this day – when we would all face death, – he had gone voluntarily with my mother to deliver themselves into the hands of the Germans. And what of my mother? Had she forgotten the terrible executions she had witnessed in Szamotuly? Why hadn't she told my father about that? Why had she gone along with him without protesting? My fear grew as I tried to work it out. As Hilary and I discussed it we became increasingly alarmed. Maybe she had told him. And maybe he had decided, as was his character, not to wait for them to come for us but to go to them direct instead.

We remembered other times when he had done this. Like the time, not so long ago, when the bandit had come to kill him. What chance could he have against these ruthless Germans? And how could he be so confident as to leave us behind in this terrible danger? It was easy for him to tell us: 'everything would be all right,' but did he really know what the Germans were like?

"Wouldn't it be better," Hilary suggested to me, "for all of us to hide in the woods until the war is over?" I agreed. In our innocence we were thinking, it would only mean a few months. How could he know the Wehrmacht commander wouldn't have them both shot on the spot, leaving us helpless for Preus and his friends to come here and kill us?

Szymon and Marie tried to reassure us that my parents knew what they were doing. That we should not be so angry and alarmed, just more patience until our parents returned. That made us angrier. I told Szymon: "Maybe if they do return, we won't be here for them any more. The Gestapo will have taken us children away and leave no evidence."

The telephone was still working and we sat close to it waiting for it to ring. It did, once, and I answered. It was only my mother's friend, Mrs. Frensko, wanting to speak to her. After that we just sat and waited. I knew Hilary was thinking the same things as I was. The clock told us it was after 20 hours since the Germans had departed yesterday. We had counted every one of them. Now in less than four hours they would be back for us, and every passing minute increased our fear and tension.

When Waldemar woke from his midday sleep I took him from his cot. Hilary and I played with him and this helped us to forget our fear. He was a beautiful baby with long blond wavy hair and Hilary and I loved him dearly. He was a happy child, always smiling. We began to wonder what would happen to him when they had executed us. We imagined awful things and, while we went on playing, we began to cry.

Suddenly Pursil became excited, and started barking, then raced outside towards our front gate. Hilary grabbed Waldemar and we rushed out after Pursil, confident from the tone of the barking that it was somebody he knew. My parents were bringing their bicycles through the side gate.

They smiled when they saw us and we knew all was well. My mother rested her bicycle against the wall and took Waldemar from Hilary into her arms.

My father also put his bike aside and began to explain what had happened with the *Wehrmachtkommander* as, one arm around each of us, he led us into the house.

"No need for us to fear today," he said.

He had explained the situation about the rifles. Neither Preus, who had been a family friend, nor anybody else had ever seen such weapons in their home, because they simply didn't exist. They had questioned him about his where-abouts over the last several weeks, how he had survived at Kutno and how he had made his way home.

"However, we had to wait several hours while they made inquiries. It seemed they were satisfied about the rifles, because they finally assured us we could return home. They would give us no assurances, however, as to how long we would be permitted to stay at our home."

Despite this, there was a new atmosphere in our house. Marie began to prepare lunch. As we sat at the kitchen table, my father explained to us what was happening all over Poland. The Russians had attacked from the east on 17 September while the Polish army was fully occupied against Germans in the west. That too was the day he had survived at Kutno.

"So the war for Poland is lost." he told us, "but Poland is not defeated. Our country will continue to resist in whatever way is possible."

The Wehrmacht commander had implied, without spelling the matter out, that our continued stay in our home would be only temporary. Soon the first Germans civilians would arrive from the Reich and all local authority, administration, and social and industrial activity would be transferred to their control. For Hilary and me, as for most Polish children, for the first time in our lives, there was no real purpose, no definable future. We did not have even a school to attend.

Despite all this and for reasons we didn't understand, our father began to repair and refurbish everything in the house and rebuild and recommission everything that had been damaged during the search of the factory. We would observe him in the afternoons taking his rosary beads and going out quietly into the forest for personal communication with

God. At night again we prayed as a family before going to bed. During these prayers, he would ask God to allow us to survive and allow him to fulfil his mission. What this mission was we didn't understand. We knew well, as did our mum, that he was a very strong character. But whatever she might have known, Hilary and I did not know, nor did we have the courage to ask him what he wanted to achieve.

Every idle day seemed to us now to be a wasted day, but idle days did not last. Four days after my father's return from his visit to the Wehrmacht commander he was visited by a high – ranking SS officer. His black uniform made me tremble as I saw him emerge from his long motor car, the door held open for him by his chauffeur, also in black SS uniform. He was very tall, maybe two metres. The chauffeur opened the wicket gate for him. Slowly, arrogantly, he strolled around the yard, clearly expecting somebody to come forth and greet him with much deference. We were all watching him through the window.

Intuitively my parents exchanged glance, realising that here was trouble. Without losing his composure, my father went out to meet him, approached him calmly and stood erect. The SS officer raised his arm and shouted: *"Heil Hitler!"* My father, in a quiet voice, responded with: *"Guten Tag."*

"Wer sind Sie denn?" the German asked imperiously.

"I am the owner," my father answered him.

"Sind Sie ein Pole, ja?"

"Ja, das bin ich, – I am a Pole."

"Well then, let me tell you that you are no longer the owner. This now is German property. However, for the time being, you will remain in charge, just so long as everything is maintained in good order and functions satisfactorily. If anything should occur to impede production, you know what to expect! Is all that clear?"

"Jawohl. It is." My father nodded, his voice still calm.

"Good." Now the German changed his tone.

"Will you now please tell me how you will recommission the plant and show me your immediate production plans?" My father turned and came back to the house and, without addressing any of us, fetched his plans from his desk and took them outside. For some time they discussed the plans, my father emphasising the importance of his newly acquired machinery and his need for other equipment.

At this point, sensing the trauma was passing, my mother decided she needed a bunch of keys which my father normally had with him. Without thinking, she sent me out to ask my father for the keys. I, also without thinking, went out, excused myself in Polish and asked for the keys.

The German froze instantly, than angrily asked my father:

"Who is this?"

"My son."

"Why doesn't he speak German?" The arrogance had returned to his voice.

"Because we speak Polish at home."

"Is that so? Well then, I'll give your boy one week to learn and speak German. I shall return and if he cannot speak German to me, he will be removed from here. On German property and German territory only German will be spoken. Also, as from now, the picture of the Führer shall be displayed in a prominent place in your home. *Einverstanden?"*

My father nodded.

The German raised his regimented arm. *"Heil Hitler!"* He turned abruptly and strode from our property to his waiting vehicle. My father came into the house and sat down. He asked my mother to bring him a glass of water and, after he had drunk it, took a deep breath before speaking. We were waiting for him to tell us what had happened but already I had the feeling that this high – ranking SS officer had sweeping powers and would be in a position to decide who remained in our area and who had to go.

My father still had the plans in his hands. He emitted a sigh indicating some relief. Then his eyes became animated. "We are staying," he announced, "and I shall get from Germany the extra machinery I need. This is what I have been working towards."

Then he motioned Hilary and me towards him and addressed us. "Boys, here is one condition that has to be met if we are to stay together. In one week, one week only, you must learn to speak and understand the German language. There is no question how. From this moment on our mother and I will speak only German in this house and will be teaching you both to do likewise. In a week from today, this same German officer will return and if we are all speaking German we shall be safe. Our lessons will be non-stop and we must start straight away."

Hilary and I well realised what would happen if we couldn't meet this demand. It was a powerful incentive. Hilary had already studied German for a year at school, but I couldn't speak a word of it. From that moment my mother began teaching us the numerals, the alphabet, German words and sentences. The lessons were intensive and continued late into the night – until we were weary and mentally exhausted. Waldemar had only to listen and caught on easily, he was that age.

I was to face the biggest problem, but not only with the learning. The repeated traumas of the past several weeks had all been too much for me. During the night four days later I felt a terrible itch in my hands. In the morning my hands were sore and raw from scratching. Next morning the itch had spread to my feet, three fingers were open and bleeding, so my mother took me to Dr. Wloh in Szamotuly.

He diagnosed eczema, caused by the disruption of my nervous system. It was a complaint that was to remain with me for over 15 years. Now I had a problem with my writing, because it was wet eczema. Each night my hands were sealed with paper bags with holes punctured in them to let air pass through to prevent me reopening the wounds. My extreme discomfort, however, did not excuse me from my intensive learning of German.

I regretted then that I had declined three years earlier when my mother offered to teach me German. Now I had no choice but to study under immense pressure.

The seventh day arrived and we continued our learning and practice until midday, until my parents decided it was time to let us rest. That day we were expecting the SS officer to return.

We didn't have long to wait. At three o'clock in the afternoon the same black Mercedes brought the same black-uniformed German SS officer with his frightening soulless arrogance.

Once again my father went out and approached him. Without even a glance in his direction my father was brushed aside. "With you I have nothing to speak. Where is your son?"

My father turned and called to me in German: "Teddy, please come here!"

I had been waiting for this, very nervously. Now the moment of truth had arrived. For the second time I was facing a black satan in human form with the power of life and death over me. Was I going to be taken away with him?

I went to the door, made the Sign of Cross as my father had taught me to do in such situation, then walked out quickly towards my father.

"Ja, bitte, Vater?"

"Der Herr will mit dir sprechen."

I took a few steps towards the SS officer. I spoke in a loud calm voice. *"Guten Tag."* I had the feeling this gave him a good impression. He asked me a few questions and, to my surprise, I felt quite relaxed. I answered his questions in perfect German. This man would be used to people cowering before him, and somehow I felt my knowledge and calmness impressed him.

He suddenly turned towards my father, raised his arm abruptly, shouted: *"Heil Hitler!"* and strode away.

After he had gone my father lifted me into his arms, hugged me and said I had done very well. For me it seemed that heaven had opened. I could not understand what had happened to me standing before that terrible man and finding that all my fear and trembling had gone.

Another ordeal was over.

C·H·A·P·T·E·R 6

Forced Evacuation

MID-OCTOBER: the days shorter and colder. We are still on our property as are the rest of our Polish neighbours who have chosen to remain. But we know it is a different story in other parts of the country and we wonder how long this will continue for us.

My father is still anxious to bring in from Germany the machinery he had paid for before the outbreak of hostilities.

One day he left for Poznan on business with my mother. Hilary and I were bored; we didn't know what to do with ourselves. (My mother had a saying: "The devil finds work for idle hands to do." How right she was.) Hilary now came with a suggestion that seemed a great idea to both of us. We would paint the hated German swastika on Waldemar's bum! After the little fellow awoke from his midday sleep, Hilary told him to take off his pyjamas and lean over the bed. He was soon into the spirit of things while I got hold of my mother's lipstick and some black shoe polish. With these primitive artist materials we soon managed to implant in red and white and black a fine detailed reproduction of the proud German emblem in what we considered a most appropriate place. Waldemar climbed off the bed while we stood back admiring our handiwork. He wanted too to see what we had painted because the black polish was beginning to itch on his bum. He climbed up onto a high stool in front of the bedroom mirror, turned his back to the mirror as he stood up, bent over and looked between his legs to survey our artwork and shrieked in delight.

"That's where the swastika belongs," Hilary told him as we helped him down and dressed him, laughing and excited at the fun of it all.

We were still enjoying our secret and Marie's ignorance of it an hour later when we observed a tall figure in a black uniform pass by our living room window outside. Abruptly our mirth drained from us, our laughter stopped and was replaced by silence, exchanged glances and a deep feeling of alarm.

We waited and, without a warning knock, our front door was thrown open. Herr Preus walked in, imperious in his black finery, and looked down coldly from one to the other of us. Hilary and I shuddered. We hadn't expected to see this evil man so soon again. What was he here for now?

"Where are your parents?" he demanded in Polish.

"They're gone to Posen," Hilary and I replied in unison. Careful to use the German form for Poznan, one trembling voice echoing the other. Our use of German surprised him.

"So!" In his new arrogance he walked over to my father's desk, sat on it and planked his black booted feet on my father's chair. "And when will they be back?" We didn't reply and, while he waited, his wandering eyes fell upon the portrait of Adolf Hitler to the side of the desk. Clearly pleased, his hand reached out and rested on it. Fearful I waited for him to reverse it and find my mother's portrait.

But at that moment little Waldemar innocently climbed on the desk and sat beside him. Waldemar's big blue eyes were glued on the red armband with its prominent swastika decorating Preus left arm. He continued to study it intensely and, after a few moments, looked up at Preus.

"*Ich habe auch ein Hakenkreutz,*" he announced innocently, mischievously.

"Oh! You have one too? Then let me see it," Preus replied.

Waldemar slumped to the floor, hands reaching to the waistband of his pants. I nearly died, but Hilary showed presence of mind and acted quickly. He grabbed Waldemar, and pushed him towards the kitchen. "You're filthy. Go and have a wash before you talk to anyone." Desperately I searched my mind, trying to distract Preus. A thought came.

"Would you like to see some of mummy's books, Herr Preus?"

"*Nein!*" He answered abruptly and turned his attention to papers on my father's desk. He picked up several of these and studied them. He studied them for a long time, almost an hour it seemed to me, with little conversation. Suddenly, finally, he stood up from the desk and left the house without further word. As soon as we knew he had left the property Hilary and I grabbed Waldemar in the kitchen, debagged him and furiously washed the swastika from his bum. We laughed when we had finished but it was bravado. We realised how close we had come to paying a heavy price for our tomfoolery.

We felt sure that Preus would have executed all three of us without a second thought.

It was late in the evening, just shortly before curfew (Poles could not be out on the streets after 10 o'clock) when our parents returned. We didn't dare tell them about the swastika but my parents were astounded that the contemptible Preus had had the gall to come again to our house.

We never saw Preus again, but later my parents learned that he had taken part in many SS atrocities before he was killed on the eastern front the day after the German offensive began on Russian occupied Poland in June 1941.

Early in November 1939 the new equipment for the fodder plant began to arrive from Germany. It was delivered in trucks in three consignments over a period of ten days, kettles, motors, presses, transmission wheels and other parts. Two bricklayers were employed to prepare the bedding before the assembling and commissioning. Frost and severe conditions, however, delayed the commissioning of the plant. It was finally ready before end of winter, the only plant of its kind in Poland producing fodder for livestock with soap as a by-product.

I heard my father mention once to my mother that everything was going according to his plan and this was giving him much satisfaction. Many delegations of German officials arrived from time to time and, observing his intensive progress expressed their own satisfaction. My father could read the German mind well! He had found a way to remain in control of his home and factory when all around us production facilities were being handed over to newly arrived civilian technicians from Germany.

From a variety of sources the news was reaching us of mass executions in the forest and mass evacuations from the towns and villages. More and more individuals, and sometimes families, would disappear without trace and relatives dared not approach German officials for information. Occasionally, after a lapse of some time, word would be volunteered that a missing relative had died of a heart attack or some other ailment and had been buried. None were convinced.

CZESLAW KAZMIERSKI BESIDE THE KENNELS

A year went by from the first attack on Poland and the oppression of the Nazi occupation got steadily worse. One September day I was walking through the forest into Brodziszewo. A convoy of German trucks overtook me and went on. There were four or five soldiers in every truck. As they went by I withdrew into the forest very frightened. This was a bad omen, and I wondered what might happen to me.

Watching from the distance I observed the trucks come to a halt in the centre of the village. The soldiers leapt from the truck with their rifles at the ready, and spread out, moving from house to house, calling out the occupants. *"Alle raus, alle raus, schnell, schnell!"* and herding residents roughly towards the trucks. This went on for some 15 minutes. These villagers were mostly peasants, farm workers and their families. Some managed to take a few personal effects and baggage with them. Many didn't.

As I watched I soon realised that this was a forced evacuation of Brodziszewo, a village of less than 500 people to which we also belonged as we lived only a kilometre or so away.

They were being crowded into the trucks with no room to move. I turned and raced back through the forest, avoiding the main pathway, to tell my parents what I had seen. I had a dreadful feeling the trucks would collect us on their way back. After a while we heard the loud singing of hymns and the barking of the German's dogs which were being used to control the villagers. My father ordered us to get into our heaviest and warmest clothes, then tried to calm my mother who was panicking and unable to decide what to pack. Soon from a distance we could hear the engines of the trucks as they came closer. My mother took Waldemar in her arms. We expected the trucks to arrive at any moment, to hear the harsh shouts of *"alle raus... raus"*. My father was showing no alarm or concern. He remained calm, stoic. I kept asking myself could he be so indifferent to what was about to happen, to where we might be taken?

I asked him in successive questions, what would happen to Szymon and Maria, what would happen to Mr. Bilski, Maluszczak and Stan, the workers at our factory. He came back with just one answer that we should not fear but trust in God. "Whatever is to happen is beyond us, there is nothing we can do."

I could no longer stand the strain. I wanted to go out to see if the trucks would turn into our place or turn off at the crossroads for Szamotuly. My father ordered me to stay inside with the rest of the family. Soon we realised the engine noises were receding. They had indeed turned off for Szamotuly! So once again we had escaped. But only for a short time I was sure. Before long they would come again for us.

Next morning I was on edge. I sneaked out into the forest and went on to Brodziszewo. I was anxious to see who was still there, in particular my friend Jenny and her family. The village was deserted. Jenny's house was deserted. Only sheep, cattle and horses remained in the yards and the stables. Without searching further I ran home, feeling very depressed.

That afternoon, once again, we could hear a convoy of trucks going towards Brodziszewo. This time, by the sound, a much larger convoy. They're going back to collect the farm animals, we thought. But no. Soon we found out that this convoy was bringing in new settlers, *Balkandeutsche*. These were Germans who lived in the Balkans since the 19th Century.

A little later we learned that the Polish inhabitants of Brodziszewo had been scattered widely, some to work in

German factories, many to the huge prison at Wronki, others sent to the General *Gubernamen*, or sent to small scattered hamlets at the edge of the forests. Those settled in the hamlets turned out to be the lucky ones because they were, in the main, forgotten about. Among them were Bilski and Maluszczak who continued to work for us at the fodder plant.

Conditions in the hamlets were cramped and primitive. One solitary room was assigned to each family irrespective of the size of the family. This had to serve as kitchen, bathroom, living room and bedroom. Bunks, sometimes three high, served as beds.

People who had jobs had no fear of further displacement. For that reason Maluszczak's daughter, Stefia, aged 16, came to work for us as a housemaid and babysitter to look after my third brother, Joachim, when he was born in 1942.

Because of the constant threat of evacuation and resettlement in villages all around us, and the chronic eczema affecting my hands, my parents decided to send me to my mother's parents in Subkowy, in Pomerania, North Poland.

My grandparents had lost their farm there but because the house was huge (seven rooms) the Germans had allowed them to occupy one room. In this cramped environment I felt quite safe but I missed my parents and was homesick. During this period the Germans continued their requisitioning of Polish farms, homes, and businesses, turning them over to the new German settlers. My parents, still at home, among the last of the Poles to still have possession of their own property, brought me back after three months and I was overjoyed to be with them again.

Clandestine Activities

IT WAS THE BEGINNING OF SPRING 1941 when I returned from my grandparents' place to 'the forest' as our home was referred to by family members and friends. Everything seemed the same as it was when I left, but I could sense that something was different, something I could not define. To me it was still the secure haven of my childhood, even allowing for the terror of the last couple of years. When there were no Germans around it remained a vibrant Polish environment, defiantly uncontaminated by the odious picture of Hitler displayed prominently on my father's desk during the daytime hours. One thing that made me feel particularly good was my return to our traditional family practice of praying together before bedtime, something I had missed at my grandfather's place.

When I got up the first morning back I was curious to find my mother finishing the packaging of dozens of parcels, mostly small but many somewhat larger. When I asked her what these were, she dismissed me with an explanation that didn't ring true. They were gifts, she told me, for relatives, for uncles, aunts and cousins I wasn't aware of, and for friends. A little later I noticed my father hiding these parcels in the back of a Citroën truck he had acquired while I was away.

All this made me suspicious. Whatever they were up to I sensed it was something secretive which I should not speak to anybody about. The truck had been purchased with the permission of the German authorities, after my father explained it was needed for the operations at the fodder plant. But its real purpose was to serve my fathers own clandestine activities, the nature of which I was not as yet aware, despite my curiosity aroused by telltale signs all around our home.

In our garage, for instance, I noticed for the first time huge rolls of heavy greaseproof paper, of a quality I have never ever seen since. There were many balls of sturdy twine near them.

I asked myself what this stuff was for. In the nights our kitchen became a hive of activity and unaccustomed smells. My mother worked herself almost to exhaustion over our coal-fired stove, frying kilo after kilo of pork fat brought from the fodder plant, making lard.

The garret of our house, under the roof, which had always been used for storage purposes, mainly of my mother's extensive books and our toys, had now been fitted out with shelves which were used for soap going through the drying process. (A similar activity, the drying of soap after manufacture, was also going on officially in an attic area above the fodder plant.) All this I observed in my first two days back.

There were, therefore, many questions I wanted to put to my parents, but some sixth sense was telling me it was not time, that I should wait.

A day or two later a heavy German motor car arrived at our home. A slim very tall man emerged from the vehicle and I felt a stab of fear. Being tall and being German, which this person clearly was, were characteristics that stamped on my mind the dreaded Gestapo.

My father immediately got up from his desk and, observing him approach at the window, told us we should treat this gentleman pleasantly and with respect; that he is a very important person.

"Important person", I was thinking, disappointed with my father. Such a tall one. For sure he is an SS officer in plain clothes, a *Sicherheitsdienst* man! Outside, my father welcomed him with unusual warmth, which I could see was genuine and was puzzled by this.

"Guten Tag, Herr Doctor." I heard him say as he stretched out his hand in greeting. The German shook his hand and immediately they turned and walked side by side, to and fro across the yard, in deep conversation for several minutes. Meanwhile my mother prepared coffee, obviously for the 'guest'. Finally my father led the stranger into the house and the first thing I noticed on his coat was the round badge of the Nazi Party: N.S.D.A.P. After greeting him we sat down to coffee.

When we had finished my father told Hilary and me to go out into the yard and play because he had important business matters to discuss with 'Herr Doctor'. I felt disturbed. I had no doubt that this man was just another Nazi official.

Two days later, a Sunday morning, my mother told me she had invited the new teacher in Brodziszewo and his family to come for afternoon coffee. Poles, I knew, no longer had the privilege of education. This new teacher would have come to look after the children of the new settlers who, we had soon come to realise, were people of much lesser intellect than the Polish peasant families they had replaced.

"They are not *Baltendeutsche*," my mother explained of the new teacher's family. They are North Germans, from Bochum near Düsseldorf."

Noticing my confusion, she took my arm and told me I should keep in mind that there were good Germans people too, who had to be careful with the authorities.

"Like Dr. Von Der Oue," she added, making the first reference to our tall slim visitor of two days before. "He is the District Veterinarian and comes from Bavaria. He is a good friend."

"Who? The tall one with the Nazi Party badge?" I was resentful.

"Yes," my mother confirmed.

"How can he be a friend if he is still a Nazi?"

"Leave it now," she said. "Your father will explain all when he has time. But I can tell you that he is a very unusual man. In time you will be convinced. Also the new teacher and his family. You can speak freely with this family. They are people we will need and we are sure they will be friends to us."

My curiosity was further aroused and for the next several hours I was waiting anxiously for the new teacher and his family to arrive. My mother mentioned they had five children, three boys of which the eldest was a Luftwaffe pilot and two daughters.

In the afternoon I was playing with a ball on the roadway outside our house when I noticed six people strolling in our direction. These I was sure must be our visitors. It pleased me to note the two boys were about the same age as Hilary and me but realised, since they were Germans, there was no real chance we could be friends. As they drew near I approached them.

"You must be Teddy then?" The man addressed me.

"*Jawohl*," I answered.

"*Ich bin Hermesmann.*" He shook my hand and turned to introduce the others.

"*Das ist meine Frau... und Kristel und Walburga, Eberhard und Georg.*"

"*Bitte, kommen Sie rein,*" I welcomed them and led the way inside.

As we sat enjoying coffee and cake and chatting at the table, my father produced some spirits and fine liqueurs from a store he had buried in a pit in the yard. Herr Hermesmann was a jovial extrovert of a man and he soon had us all relaxing and laughing.

It was a long time since I had seen my parents laugh; it was good to see them laughing again. Eberhard, who was Hilary's age, and I shared immediate rapport but Georg was only nine, nearly two years younger than me, and I saw him as just a kid.

They left about six in the evening and, at the door, Herr Hermesmann invited us to come to their place next time. In a whisper he said to my father: "We can listen together to the BBC in London."

We stood and watched them as they walked away towards Brodziszewo, called now Sahsenhoff, then, as my mother and Hilary returned to the house, my father asked me to go with him for a walk in the forest because he had been sitting for too long.

The prospect of walking once again with my father in the forest filled me with pleasure. It had been nearly two years since we had walked together. In that time we had suffered much, but not alone. We witnessed terror and tragedy all around us.

I loved the forest. After three months away in Subkowy, surrounded by flat country in which I could never quite feel secure, I really missed the forest. Once again I felt proud and safe walking here with my father. We could see owls looking down on us from the trees and could hear birdsong fading into the evening.

After a little while my father began explaining to me the terrible effects the war was having on the Polish people. The rationing system gave them little to eat and most were suffering severely from hunger.

"We cannot observe all this with indifference, Teddy. God is looking after us. We still have enough to eat and we have been allowed to stay here, but it will only remain so as long as we do as much as possible to help other people in need."

"As long as we are helping people in need," he repeated solemnly, "so long will God protect us and permit us to stay here in safety. We all have a role to fulfil in this life, Teddy. An important person to all of us is Dr.Von Der Oue. I met him only recently. He is an extraordinary man, with great character and courage, who is prepared to selfishly endanger his own life to help the Polish people. We need him and for sure in the future we will meet other Germans like him. Otherwise we won't survive."

"Remember, Teddy, you must be very careful. Whatever you may see happening in our home, you must not tell anyone, anyone at all. Only Hilary, your mum and I know anything about this. Not Waldemar. Not even he must know what is going on. He is too young to understand and therefore a danger to all of us. If the German want to learn something, it is Waldemar they will ask first."

"So remember: you have seen nothing and heard nothing."

Altogether we spent about an hour in the forest and then with darkness falling we turned for home. Walking in silence, I pondered how much things had changed in the three months I had been away. I had a new perspective on our lives.

'Fixing' a Pole

A MAELSTROM OF TROUBLED THOUGHTS crowded my head throughout the night so that I could not sleep. The real nature of my father's mission, towards which he had been working and directing the family's prayers, was at last clear to me. I had wondered many times since the German had arrived if he realised the dangers he was exposing all of us to through his activities. I knew he was not reckless or indifferent, but I also knew of people, indeed of whole families, who had been brutally killed for minor misdemeanors or breaches of the strict regulations the Germans had imposed on us.

Just a few days later I witnessed at close hand the mindless thuggery of some of the German police *(Schutzpolizei)* who at times seemed to lose their sanity in an abyss of sadism. I was strolling along the path to the forest and, at a point where it crossed the main road about 200 metres from my home, a bus pulled up and a short burly policeman alighted. He stood for a moment in front of me, looking down with a friendly expression, hands on hips, then asked what I was doing in the forest.

"I live here," I told him in German.

"*Ach so!*" he nodded appreciatively. "Well I'm on duty here for a while, would you like to keep me company?"

I thought it better not to refuse. Anyway he seemed intelligent and civilised. I went with him, sure that he thought I was German. He would be aware that there were no Poles now left in Brodziszewo. I didn't make conversation, not anxious to be questioned, and noticed two cyclists approaching. Workmen. As they came near I could see they were Poles, because of the regulation white stripe which all Poles were required to have on their bicycles. I sensed somehow there might be trouble here, so I distanced myself a little from him. As they came abreast of us they doffed their caps, quickly, nervously. This was another requirement imposed on Poles whenever they passed a German.

"*Halt!*" He stopped them and stepped close to the nearest man.

Without explanation or warning he raised clenched fists and struck the man viciously, first on the right, then the left side of the head. The man staggered sideways, blue discolouration appearing on his face.

"Next time remember to salute a German properly," he barked and ordered him to move on, at the same time indicating to the other to stay.

Now he approached the second Pole and enquired where he was going.

"*Zu Arbeit,*" the man answered hesitantly in imperfect German.

"What have you got in that bag."

"My lunch for the day."

"Open it. Show me!"

The man opened the small lunch bag and produced two pieces of sliced bread and two eggs. The German's bulging eyes focussed on the eggs. He extracted a notebook from his pocket and ordered the Pole to put his bike to one side. The man obeyed and returned the food to the lunch bag. The German continued to write in his notebook. He finished then called the Pole forward to sign the report.

As the man completed his signature and made to return the notebook, the German raised both fists and struck him solidly in the eyes. The Pole reeled and the policeman went on to him fists flailing. At this point I was terrified, standing about 15 metres away. I could only stare. The man was trying to protect his face with his arms. Blood was spurting from his nose. He made no attempt to retaliate as the German continued his brutal attack, yelling loudly at him. "You are only allowed one egg to work. What for the second egg? Are you giving it to somebody?"

The man made no reply. His face was covered in blood. The German policeman continued to punch him until he fell to the ground. Then the German, his uniform spattered with the other's blood, began to kick him viciously. He continued to kick him for several minutes, the blood now spattering his leather boots.

Suddenly the Pole went limp. I saw he was unconscious, maybe dead. I half expected the German to remove his revolver and shoot the prone figure. He didn't but continued to kick him mercilessly – in the stomach, in the back, in the lungs, in the head, his face contorted with pleasure, teeth showing in laughter, eyes bulging. Kick... kick... kick... he began to tire, stopped, breathing heavily, and smiled again, pleasurably surveying the broken blood – covered object of his brutality. Finally, his eyes focussed on his own bloodied hands, and the blood staining his uniform and boots. He turned towards me.

"Take me to where you live, *Junge*. I must clean this mess from my clothes."

Looking at him I shivered. The blood had even spattered his face. I wished it was his own blood but no, it was the blood of that poor hopeless man at his feet. Half dazed, I turned and led him towards my home. I couldn't speak.

From the window my mother observed us approaching. She was waiting inside the door as we entered. Very politely the policeman excused his dishevelled and bloodied condition.

"Official duty, madam," he explained with a smile. He'd had to 'fix a Pole', he told her, clearly assuming she was German.

"I couldn't return to the police station in this condition, may I, please clean up."

Without speaking my mother turned and led him to the trough in the kitchen. Silently she nodded to it, then turned and left him. It was some time before he finally emerged. Then my mother asked him coldly: "Where have you come from?"

"I am from Otorowo," he told her, "But now I am stationed in Szamotuly. I spent last night in Otorowo and met a very fine police colleague, a head or two taller than me," he added with a chuckle.

My mother nodded. Even from that brief description she felt she knew the person he was referring to.

"That would be Herr Hard, I expect."

"*Jawohl!*" His face beamed. "Herr Hard, a very fine gentleman. You know him?"

"*Natürlich.* I have heard a lot about him." Indeed she had.

"Yes? Good. Actually he was telling me he would soon have solved the Polish problem in this area. His plans are well in hand." My mother made no comment.

"Now that I am in Szamotuly," he continued, "I shall have to perform well to reach the status of respect that Herr Hard enjoys here."

He asked for a drink and my mother brought him a glass of water. He drank it lustily and returned the glass. A smile spread over his piggish face, he clicked his booted heels together and raised his right arm. *"Heil Hitler!"* he shouted, then turned and left, blissfully confident he had been enjoying the brief hospitality of a German home. Two minutes later my father came into the house, his expression concerned.

"Go after him, Teddy, and see what he is doing. See if he gets on the bus and what direction. Then see if that other poor fellow is still on the ground. We must help him."

I went out and could see the brute in the distance, waiting at the crossroads. As I watched he stepped forward and hailed a passing car. The vehicle stopped and he climbed in. It moved on again in the direction of Szamotuly. I went on out to the roadway to see if the injured workman was still lying where we had left him. There was no sign of him. Other people, Poles I hoped, must have carried him away. I went home and told my father.

I was still shaken by the brutality of the man and couldn't get him out of my mind. Then my thoughts turned to the one he had spoken about. I asked my mother: "Who is this fine gentleman, Herr Hard, and how do you know about him?"

She glanced at me and her expression was cautioning.

"Don't even think about him, Teddy. It would be better if you knew nothing about him."

"He has been here when you were away," my father broke in, obviously thinking I should be told more.

"A highly intelligent man but nonetheless a ruthless beast, unscrupulous, without a semblance of decency. We can only thank God that, as yet, this family has experienced no evil at his hands. The Polish people here call him 'Hardy'. Many have suffered dearly through him and many more have disappeared without trace."

"His favourite Sunday sport," my father continued, "is to stand at the side door of the church in Otorowo, the only one the people are allowed to use after mass. As they come out, this Herr Hard, with the help of a couple of his colleagues, wades into them with his baton, injuring as many as possible. This can go on for up to 20 minutes, until he and his friends get tired and give up."

Here he took a deep breath to relieve his mounting anger.

"There's a just God in heaven who will not allow this to go on for long. He will be punished."

At this point my father went to his desk, opened the top drawer and came back holding a newspaper cutting.

"This is from the *'Ostdeutscher Beobachter'*," (East German Observer) he said and began to read extracts from a speech by Hitler. The Führer was exhorting the entire German nation to destroy ruthlessly the spirit of Poland, in particular its Catholic faith.

"Unless we can destroy the Polish faith in God," my father read out, "we shall never totally destroy Poland."

This puzzled me and I protested: "But the German soldiers wear belts with buckles that say: *'Gott mit uns'*. So how can Hitler ask his soldiers to fight against God? Why are they closing our churches? Why are they destroying all the crosses and statues and the headstones in our graveyards?"

My father shook his head and his smile was rueful.

"Teddy, it will be hard for you to understand this. It is beyond the understanding of somebody your age. Hitler has beside him people who carry out his most barbaric orders with enthusiasm and efficiency under the labels of God and

Christianity. That is why they will never win this war, even if they take over the whole world. Because those who fight against God cannot win."

He left me to ponder this, returned the cutting to his desk and went out.

C·H·A·P·T·E·R 9

"What is it about you that makes all this possible?"

H ITLER'S *'BLITZKRIEG'* (Lightning War) had achieved its first objective in Eastern Europe, the conquest of Poland exclusive of the regions which had fallen to the Soviet Union following the agreement reached between the two foreign ministers, Von Ribentrop and Molotov.

In the defeated Poland the Germans had been selectively transporting the bulk of the Polish workforce and healthy younger people westward into Germany to serve as slave labour in the factories and farms of the Third Reich.

In Eastern Poland, on the other hand, the Soviet aggressors moved entire families in vast numbers East into the Urals and beyond to Siberia.

At home Hitler's volatile speeches were emphasising more and more the German need for *'Lebensraum'* (living space for the economic and social progress of the German Reich).

He was clearly focussing on the vast territories to the East, although no public mention was made of the Soviet Union. Stalin, however, was being constantly warned of

Hitler's real intention by the western allies. But the Soviet dictator was playing for time while he won the support of the Soviet masses which he had been suppressing so ruthlessly.

On 22 June 1941 Hitler launched his 'Operation Barbarossa', the invasion of the Soviet Union by his vast and powerfully equipped Panzer Divisions, the Wehrmacht, and the Luftwaffe. Daily now the East German Observer, carried stories of the huge successes of the German armies on all fronts but among the Polish people there was a growing awareness of widespread resistance to the German occupation. Sabotage was on everybody's mind.

At our home in the forest, discussing these events, my father would continuously express his conviction that the disposition of the German armies over so wide a front and the barbaric suppression of the people in the territories they occupied signalled the beginning of the end for Hitler. He would tell us, "Napoleon's army froze to their deaths in the depths of Russia. The same will happen to the Germans, if not this first winter then certainly the following year. This war will not last much beyond that." His words gave all of us renewed hope.

By the end of summer my father was bringing home intermittent copies of a Polish underground newsletter 'Polska Walczaca' (Poland Fighting). All the family would read this with much interest. We could retain it for no more than a day, as it had to be passed on to others. Also to be caught in possession of it meant death.

The day after he brought home the first issue I was told to take it to my father's friend, Mr. Kaczmarek in Lipnica, some 3 kilometres away. I knew the Kaczmarek family well. Their son Wladyslaw was, at this time, my best friend. My mother sewed a small bag to hold the newsletter and stitched it inside my trousers on the left side. With the newsletter concealed there, my father gave me a German newspaper to carry it in my hand. I took a short cut through the forest towards Lipnica where Mr. Kaczmarek was a supervisor in a (German) state-controlled distillery and farm. I came out of the forest at a point where the main road bordered a pond and walked straight into a group of six Hitler Youth on bicycles, all of them a few years older than me.

They dismounted immediately, gathered around me and began to throw questions at me; where I lived, where I was going and so on. Although I spoke German, they realised quickly that I was a *'Polak'* and became aggressive. Dropping their bicycles, they closed in around me and began pushing me from one to another.

I realised I was in grave danger. It would only be a matter of minutes until they found the newsletter. The pushing got rougher and then they began to punch me. My body was hurting and suddenly I received a heavy punch on the side of the head and fell down. Now they began to kick me and the kicking became more vicious until a heavy boot struck me suddenly in the mouth and I lost consciousness.

It must have been a couple of hours later when I came to. I didn't know where I was.

After a while I could see I was lying in a drain beside the road but I couldn't remember what had happened to me. Then I felt the sour taste of blood in my mouth and when I spat out the blood I realised I had lost several teeth. I got to my knees and put my hand in my trouser pocket to find a handkerchief – and felt the newsletter my mother had sewn there.

That brought everything back. I climbed to my feet and staggered over to the pond and, using my handkerchief, cleaned the blood from my face and clothes.

The Kaczmarek home, which had become almost a second home to me, was about 500 metres further on. Now I avoided the main road and took a secluded route behind the houses.

As I climbed the stairs to the Kaczmarek's back door, Mrs. Kaczmarek came out and was shocked at my bloodied and dishevelled state... I explained to her what had happened. She brought me in, ran a bath for me and insisted I go to bed. I could go home tomorrow.

I had stayed overnight there before: she knew my parents wouldn't worry.

A week later Eberhard Hermesmann visited us in the forest and was shocked at the bruises on my arms, legs and body. My lips were still swollen and I had lost two teeth. I was reluctant to tell him what had happened, knowing that he too belonged to the *'Hitler Jugend'* but he insisted I tell him all. He listened carefully and I had the impression he felt ashamed.

At first he said nothing, then he muttered: *'Die Schweine'* under his breath. He asked me to describe them, saying he thought some of them might belong to his group. He explained that constant pressure was being put on them to provoke the Poles whenever they could. "They are not required", he told me, "to answer for anything they do against the Poles. For any abuse of that kind they can only expect to be complimented or promoted by their superiors." I wondered at him admitting all this to me. After all, I too was supposed to be his enemy.

From this time on our friendship deepened. I knew he avoided meetings and activities of the Hitler Youth, even though membership was for him compulsory. Only once have I seen him in the uniform. He hated it and wore it only to meetings. He wasn't welcome in the organisation because of his reluctance to engage in 'anti-Pole' activities. It was only a matter of time, he told me, until he was expelled.

Eberhardt was well aware that our close fraternisation could be disastrous for him but was determined that it should continue.

A short time later he brought his eldest brother Fritz to meet us. Fritz was a *'Luftwaffe'* pilot, flying a *'Torpedo Flug-zeuge'*. Fritz was home on recuperation leave. He had been shot down and, when rescued after two days in the water, was in a very weak condition. Fritz too became a close friend of our family. He was very likeable with a happy disposition. Relatively isolated in his specialist *'Luftwaffe'* role, he had little knowledge of the widespread abuse of the Polish population.

In 1943 his parents received the news that Fritz was missing in action. Devastated, the family came to us, their only real friends, for comfort. His mother was deeply affected at the loss of her eldest and made her contempt for the Nazi regime obvious. She was unforgiving. When my father told her she should not lose hope, that God would protect her son, she was not consoled.

As they stood up to leave for their home she was crying bitterly. She put her head on my father's shoulder and asked him to pray for her son's return, saying she herself did not have the faith to pray. From that time on my father included Fritz in our family prayers each evening.

A year passed without further news of Fritz and the Hermesmann family had given up hope. Not so my father. He would insist on encouraging them to be optimistic and keep faith.

Then one day the Hermesmanns, who had not been around for some time, arrived at our place, clearly elated and smiling.

"What's all this about?' my father greeted them.

1948

My mother, Klara Kazmierski, in 1948

"Fritz is alive: we've heard from him," Frau Hermesmann burst out.

They remained with us until very late in the night. Before they left Herr Hermesmann confessed to my father that, because he lacked faith in God, he had long since given up hope but his wife had remained convinced that my father's prayers would be answered and that Fritz would return.

"What lies in you that makes your faith so strong?" he asked my father.

"I know there are things going on here on your property in defiance of the laws of the German Reich which would mean the ultimate penalty for you if found out. And yet you are still the only Polish family I know to continue in possession of your own property – while you work secretly to help your people. What is it about you that makes all this possible. I don't have the faith to understand."

My father showed no reaction and made no reply...

Herr Hermesmann then told my father he should continue with his work, "Because, I believe, for Hitler, the war is already lost."

At the end of January 1943, Eberhard, then 15, was called up and sent to the Russian front. This indicated that his observation that the *'Hitler Jugend'* did not trust him was correct. As a young soldier of the Wehrmacht, he was now serving as a *'Luftwaffenhelfer'*. Clearly somebody had wanted to get rid of him.

Hilary and I had lost a good friend with whom we had much in common. We wondered if we would see him again?

The European tragedy was at its darkest in 1943.

My mother's sister was sent to work in Germany, her husband, Edmund Sikorski, to the Mauthausen concentration camp. The youngest sister, Isabella, was removed to a concentration camp at Stuthoffen near Gdansk.

My father could see the situation was deteriorating. He knew the Germans could not continue to allow a Pole to remain in charge of a production facility on his own property.

Our friend, Dr. Von Der Oue warned us constantly and brought us information of the German administration's plans for us. He did all he could to maintain the situation at 'the forest' but in the end could not stop the inevitable. He came one day and warned us to be prepared for the worst. My father decided we should separate as a family to give some of us better hope of survival. Taken together to a concentration camp, not one of us would have much hope of survival. Waldemar, then five years old, and Hilary, 16, were sent to a small forester's lodge, deep in the forest a couple of kilometres away.

I was sent again to my grandparents in Subkowy. I had no idea that this time how long we would be separated. If I believed my father it would not be for long.

Also my mother was pregnant. She told me, to make my departure easier, that when I returned our family would be larger. "I might have a sister for you," she said.

My mother travelled with me on the train to Subkowy. We were laden with food parcels made up to look like small gifts. She warned me, on our way to the station at Szamotuly, that we would board the section of the train reserved for Germans. There we were much less likely to be harassed by the police but we had to be able to pass ourselves off as Germans.

"Remember, we shall speak only German and read German papers and magazines."

She then surprised me by putting on a badge of the German Women's Association. I wondered where she might have got the badge.

During the seven-hour journey we didn't speak much but my mother conversed constantly with the German passengers. At station stops I would wander out into the corridor, looking to see into which carriages the German police were going. I felt uneasy in this German environment and wished we were in the Polish carriages.

At one station I noticed police escorting Polish passengers into a railway building. I had a fair idea of what those poor people had to expect.

I was relieved when we arrived at my grandparents' place but next day my mother returned home. Two weeks later I received a letter from her saying she would be back to pick me up soon.

In Subkowy there were only few Polish families left and I felt like an outcast. I didn't belong there and I was missing my parents, my brothers, my friends Eberhard and Wladek, and everything that was familiar and dear to me in the security of the forest.

In this farming district of Subkowy the houses stood alone, separated 500 metres and more from the neighbouring homes and standing starkly alone in their flat open fields. It was all very unreal to me.

The main road was also 200 metres from my grandparents' house and 500 metres beyond was the railway line. Some 100 trains passed by daily but, despite my fascination with trains, nothing could take the place of my beloved forest which every season showed a different face with its changing trees and vegetation. The pleasant memories I had left behind were constantly with me: here there was no place to express my dreams.

I had my own special books, five or six of them, which I used to read in the forest.

Also in the forest, with Eberhard and Wladek, I used to build hiding places from fallen timber and moss. If the

Germans had discovered the damage we were doing to the trees and vegetation in this time of war our punishment would have been severe, something we had no wish to dwell upon. For Eberhard it might well have meant death, because he was a German fraternising with Poles.

I remember one occasion when we had built a large shelter and were feeling very self-satisfied because we had finished it in a day. The next day a Nazi Party barracks was being opened for *Reichsarbeitsdienst Mädchen* (RAD for young German women who had arrived to help on the land).

We had organised a party to celebrate the opening of what we called 'our Party house', and this was attended by my parents, the Hermesmanns and our close friends. The music from the brass band, playing for the official Party House opening in Brodziszewo, reached us in the forest and we used that music to embellish our own 'official opening'.

Two months passed in Subkowy without news from my parents. This puzzled me. My mother loved to write long letters so I thought she must be very busy and forgave her. But why she could not send a short letter disappointed me.

Everyday I waited for the postman, hoping for some news. Then finally her letter arrived, assuring me that all was well and that I could soon return home. This made me wonder what all the fuss had been about that caused us to be separated in the first instance.

A week later she arrived again laded with food parcels. I went to bed about 10 o'clock that night but was awakened several times by a long discussion between my mother and her parents that carried on into the early hours.

This time on the way home we travelled in the Polish section of the train. We were no longer carrying contraband

and felt more at ease in the company of our own people, but frequently the Gestapo and the railway police made random checks among the passengers.

In a siding at Bydgoszcz (Bromberg) railway station we saw a goods train loaded with Russian prisoners, their gaunt faces, frightened eyes and shaven heads protruding at high-set openings.

We could hear them speaking and I wondered if they knew where they were going or what to expect. All around the station were propaganda posters, telling us: 'Wheels must keep turning for victory' and 'The enemy is listening'.

At Poznan station we had a long delay. The platforms were thronged with soldiers and the pace of activity was hectic.

When we finally arrived at Szamotuly we were one-and-a-half hours late. The waiting room at the bus station was thronged with both Poles and Germans. When the bus arrived there was a rush to climb inside. It filled quickly with many standing and then the *Schutzpolizist* arrived yelling: "Poles out!" *"Alle Polaken raus!"* Priority for the Germans as always. My mother and I got out with the rest of the Poles who had managed to get in. It was two hours before the next bus arrived but finally we were on our way to 'the forest'.

The first bus stop, two kilometres on, was opposite a large park with tall iron entrance gates. A notice on these gates warned: "Dogs and Poles prohibited". A little further on, as the bus rounded a bend, a group of Hitler Jugend stood by the roadside with their bikes lying in the ditch. Clearly they were bent on making trouble for wayfarers.

"You must beware of this spot," my mother whispered to me. "Whenever you are doing errands for your father. The 'HJ' and the police are always here causing trouble for the

Poles." Finally, above the trees tops, I could see our tall chimney stack and instantly felt relieved and secure. Shortly we would be home safe and sound. I thanked God.

When we arrived home my mother cooked me a meal and I went straight to bed, exhausted after the long day. Next morning the early sunlight coming in shafts through the window shutters awakened me. The rest of the household was still sleeping so I just lay there, planning my day, my first day home, with some anticipation.

About six o'clock my father climbed from his bed and opened the shutters, filling the room with light. A warm sunny day promised.

Looking around the room I noticed something strange. There were marks on the walls I had never seen before, marks that looked like specks of blood. I wondered what might have caused them but I didn't ask my parents. When I got up I investigated the other walls in the house but they seemed unmarked.

After breakfast I went out to look around the yard to see if anything had changed during my absence. I finally wandered into the boiler room and found a bricklayer at work, finishing what looked like a new brick structure under the boiler. From there I strolled out to the kennels to see how the dogs were and after that made my way out into the forest.

The forest was like a magnet to me: I loved it and felt secure there. I went deep inside to investigate my favourite haunts and find again the shelters of branches I had built with my two close friends, Eberhard and Wladek. They were much as I had last seen them with perhaps a little extra growth around them.

I felt at home in the forests: it was where I belonged. There would be no odious German uniforms in the forest.

It was unsafe for them. But for me it was a haven, a secure hiding place. I knew it so well, its flora and its fauna and its sounds.

I wished I could join the partisans who were now using the forests effectively to harass the Germans. Then I would happily spend every night and every day in the forests. But I had no idea where the partisans were, although I was aware before I left of their growing activity. I went home for lunch then quickly returned and, using the safe route of the forest, made my way to Lipnica to Wladek's house. I had missed him while I was away. Since Eberhard's departure to the Eastern front – he was the only real friend I had left.

Wladek with his mother and sister gave me a great welcome. Mrs. Kaczmarek threw her arms out and embraced me.

"Teddy, how lucky you are to be back with your parents. Only God could have brought about this miracle – to have your parents returned from the camp."

Her words surprised me. I had no idea what she was talking about.

"What camp?" I asked her.

She could see my confusion and answered:

"Don't you know what happened? When did you get home, Teddy?"

"Yesterday,"

"Oh then, your parents will tell you all about it. They were taken away to a camp and a German family put in your home. But your parents will tell you."

Curious now, I returned home after spending a little time with the Kaczmareks, although I had told my parents I would probably stay overnight. Again I took the route through the forest, having learned from Eberhard that the *'Hitler Jugend'* were not likely to enter the forest. My mother was preparing supper and my father was already eating. She asked how the Kaczmareks were and added: "We weren't expecting you till tomorrow. You haven't seen them for three months." Then she saw there was something also on my mind.

"Has Mrs. Kaczmarek told you what happened?"

"Yes. Something, but..."

"What else do you want to know?"

"I want to know from you what happened. Why were you taken away? Who took over this house? What about those blood spots on the wall in the bedroom? Why am I told nothing?"

There was a prolonged silence. Then finally my mother answered.

"It was never likely that we would escape the fate of the other Poles around us here. We could only remain as long as it suited the Germans to keep the production going on here. But Dr. Von Der Oue warned us our deportation was coming and that's why your father sent you away."

Through all of this my father continued with his meal. Now, finishing, he turned and interrupted to take up the story.

"A German truck arrived in our yard one morning with a German family and all their wordly belongings, including rolled-up bedding. There was husband, wife and twenty-year old son who should have been in the army but seemingly had some disability. We were told to get our belongings on to the truck, – that we were being moved. I was given a couple of hours to induct the husband into the running of the fodder plant."

"They told us they had been brought here against their will. In the early afternoon we were driven away and after about three hours were deposited in a holding camp."

"Things didn't look good for us. Trucks arrived at the camp each day with more despondent Polish families, forcibly removed from their homes and villages."

"We were in the camp about ten days," my father continued, "when a truck arrived and I was amazed to see, among those who were brought in, the same German family who had taken over our place. They looked stunned, frightened. While your mother and I were talking about this, we were approached by the camp guards, taken from the enclosure and without explanation – ordered into the truck. Shortly afterwards the truck drove off."

"We had no idea where we were being taken: we had been told nothing. After about two hours I began to recognise landmarks. It seemed they were taking us back to Brodziszewo. Sure enough, we finally arrived back home here and were told to get the plant back into production without delay."

He drew a breath and looked at me, his eyes very serious.

"In all of this, Teddy, I see the working of God on our lives. We must continue to pray.

We must pray also for that German family. Their fate in that camp, in all probability, will have been worse than that of the Poles."

"Why? What happened with them?" I asked him. "I don't understand."

"They were brought here against their will. It was obvious to me the husband had no technical knowledge. In the short time I was given with him, he couldn't learn much."

"It seems in about a week he managed to wreck the boiler and bring the production process to a halt. There is no doubt the authorities interpreted this as sabotage."

"That family will have been treated more severely than we were. God help them."

Clearly my parents felt they had given me enough information because there was a long pause before my father finally said: "That's enough for now. What's past is past. What matters is the future. We have to thank God for bringing us back to our home and reuniting us."

Later my mother told me: "That poor German family left our home in a filthy condition. The blood you saw on the walls was from the bed bugs when we squashed them. But these bugs may be a blessing in disguise and save us from been deported again. While they're around nobody will want to come in here. They give your father no peace but not everybody is affected by them."

You may be lucky. We can't get rid of them because we have no killer sprays or disinfectant. But they're not causing a health problem."

I found it hard to sleep that night, waiting for them to bite. At dawn when the light crept in through the living room window I could see them on the walls. But, as it turned out, I was lucky. They didn't affect me.

Things brightened further for me a few days later when my father promised to get me a bike. "But you'll have to wait a little while," he cautioned, "because the parts will have to be got together from different places."

There was more good news to come.

The newspapers were now reporting that some Poles would be allowed to attend German schools. To my father this was an indication that the German political position was weakening.

Up to this time Polish children had been denied education. They were seen to have no future in the Third Reich except as labourers. They could be taught to count to 500 but not to read or write.

Since I had long since learned to read and write in German, this news was not particularly significant for me. But the opportunity to mix once again with young Polish people of my own age was. However I had to wait a while: the German schools were still on holidays.

Then in mid-July my parents were notified that from 1 September 1943 they must send me to the German school at Lipnica. That was only six weeks away.

C·H·A·P·T·E·R 10

My First Assignment

IT WAS SUMMER OF 1943 and I noticed that something had changed at our home in the forest. A new tempo had emerged and the entire plant had become a hive of activity.

My father, after the family had come home from the labour camp, set about rectifying the damage done during his absence. All his equipment had to be repaired and recommissioned so that maximum production could be resumed as quickly as possible. Bricklayers and metalworkers arrived and were busy. The main kettle had been cracked and rendered useless. Before work on its repair could start the brickwork around it had to be demolished. Spare parts were near impossible to find but, since it was important to the war effort, the German authorities would brook no excuses. What was needed had to be found and no bureaucratic obstruction was tolerated.

Gradually trucks began arriving from the rail depot at Szamotuly with coal fuel which elsewhere was simply not available. Even my father's old Citroën received attention.

A year earlier it had been converted to wood fuel which left it slow moving and inefficient. Now it was converted again, this time to LPG. Two LPG bottles affixed to the sides gave it a range of 500 kilometres. Because of it vintage and hard usage it was a car with dozens of problems and I was at a loss to understand why it was given so much attention. I was to learn it still had a vital role to play in my father's scheme of things.

Szymon too was given new responsibilities, first to convert our run-down and neglected yard to a model of cleanliness and order. On my father's instructions the 200 metres of laneway, leading from main road into our place, was widened, upgraded and covered with slag from the plant which was then bedded down for traffic.

My father got a permit to build a new shed which would provide larger garage space, house three horse-drawn vehicles and store hay and straw for the horses. This permit covered the collection of bricks from demolished houses in the near vicinity which had to be cleaned for re-use.

The authorities, it seemed, were impressed by my father's efforts which were conveyed to them in detail by the kindly veterinarian, Dr. Von Der Oue. He recommended that all needed permits be issued to my father – and his recommendations carried the weight of a respected Party official. Dr. Von Der Oue became a regular guest at our home. He was disciplined, hard-working and we held him in high esteem. Whenever his dark blue German-built Wanderer sedan turned from the main road into our home it had the effect of raising our spirits. He may have been German and a Party member but for all that we trusted him as a friend and protector. He was genial but rarely smiled or showed emotion. We had the feeling he was burdened by some internal stress although he never complained about his health.

My mother would invite him in for tea, coffee and cake or scones when she was able to provide them. He would discuss his wife and his son at the front and once expressed the wish that the war would soon be over. Always, after some 30 minutes, he would walk outside into the yard with my father and there, alone together, they would have long discussions in undertones.

❧

The news that my parents had been returned to our home spread quickly throughout the Szamotuly neighborhood. One morning, hours before daybreak, I emerged from a deep sleep with the feeling that somebody had been tapping on the shutters outside our bedroom window. As if in response to this my father climbed from his bed and went out to the kitchen window which also faced the forest. I got the impression my father was whispering to somebody outside but didn't take too much notice and went back to sleep. However, when the same thing happened the next morning, and the following, I became curious. On the fourth morning I sneaked out after my father, saw him speak through the window to an old woman and then hand her a parcel. I could see her glancing cautiously to the left and right, then grasp the parcel and disappear into the forest.

Next others, all elderly women, began to arrive individually at the window. They would ask for small items, mostly for pork fat or for soap. He had such parcels ready and refused nobody.

He told me later when he realised I was observing him that these women had come from as far as 15 kilometres away in the Szamotuly district to seek morsels for their families. They would travel back through the forest along the cart tracks with the parcels hidden under their skirts. On their way they collected firewood, a ploy to put off guard the German police and soldiers who might accost them.

It seemed to work but there were risks involved for my father because all of these women were strangers to him. If any were searched and gave him away it could have meant death for all of us.

As the days went by and I became accustomed to these early arrivals at our kitchen window I became enthralled with this clandestine activity. Because my father showed no indication of worry I stopped worrying. But with my mother it was a different story. She worried constantly and it showed in her face and as the months went by its effect was telling. She was finding it harder and harder to live with the impending danger.

One morning my father told me that the bike was ready, that I should go into town and collect it. That was a happy day for me: no other Polish boy that I knew had a bike. My father had to go to the Police, advise them that we had a bike, provide the frame number and confirm that the frame was painted white, a requirement for all bikes in the possession of Poles. He also had to explain that the bike was needed for me to ride into town to collect spare parts and other incidentals required to keep the plant operating.

For the first two days I revelled in riding into the forest and spending hours gaining expertise in handling my new bike. But on the third day the bike had to be put to good use.

I was instructed to take three parcels to Mr. Fresko in Szamotuly.

Mr. Fresko lived in an attic room on the third floor of a large house located in the Market Place. He had a small dog, a Chihuahua, which was a very special kind of watchdog. He was able to distinguish Germans from Poles, whatever they were wearing, and would bark incessantly whenever a German official arrived at the entrance on the ground floor. This gave Mr. Fresko the opportunity to prepare for a visit – and to conceal what had to be concealed.

That was the first of many such assignments for me. I never knew exactly what was in the parcels I carried on my bike – I suspected most likely food or soap – but I knew what I was doing was illegal. Always, before I would leave the house on an assignment, my father insisted that I make the Sign of the Cross and an aspiration to God to protect me.

I was not afraid although I knew I had to be careful. The Germans were ever watchful. And gradually my assignments became more and more frequent – to different addresses in Szamotuly and to the Post Office.

At home during the nights my mother's duty was to prepare the contents of the parcels. My father would do the parcelling, in grease-proof paper, and he was an expert at this. My task was to pick out from the papers and other sources the names of German soldiers serving (and sometimes killed) on the Eastern Front and to prepare labels for the parcels with these names, then to mark them in large lettering: 'An die Ostfront'. If, on my deliveries, I was apprehended I was to explain that the parcels were for serving soldiers at the front. Sometimes the addresses were fictional and I wondered for how long this subterfuge would work.

My father assured me constantly that if I were caught and in danger God would protect me. I believed him.

One afternoon on my way to Szamotuly with six parcels I was confronted by two German Schutzpolizei. I had a dreadful feeling that this would mean the end for me and my family. The white frame of the bike indicated I was Polish and the six parcels aroused their suspicions. First they laughed and mocked me, and then became serious. *"An die Ostfront?"* They spoke in a German dialect I was not familiar with and questioned me, surprised that I, a Pole, spoke such good German and carried parcels for soldiers at the front.

I explained that my mother was always collecting clothing and similar for the soldiers, as the newspapers were constantly asking the population to do. Deep inside I was praying they would not examine the parcels which, whatever they contained, would not be clothing.

One policeman told me to come with him while the other remained on duty where he stood.

I accompanied him, pushing the bicycle along Railway Terrace towards the Market Place where the police headquarters were located. Was this the end then? Head down I reflected on my father and his promise. Would God protect me?

We were about 200 metres from the police headquarters when the policeman suddenly pulled on my arm bringing the bike on to the footpath and instructing me to rest it against the wall. I realised it was the wall of the Post Office building. He collected three of the parcels and told me to take the other three. Inside, at the parcel window, the Polish workers knew who I was and what my father was up to. They accepted the parcels but I knew these parcels would never see the Eastern Front. They would go instead to needy Poles in the Szamotuly area. With a feeling of much relief I handed over the appropriate postage money.

As we emerged the policeman turned to me: "Go home now quickly," he said, "And tell your mother the soldiers at the front will be grateful for what she is doing."

My only concern on the way home was that I would run into one of the bands of Hitler Youth who wandered the roads harrassing, bashing and sometimes killing young Poles. I was lucky this time and later confided only to my father what had happened. For my mother it would have only increased the burden of worry she was carrying.

C·H·A·P·T·E·R 11

Ugly Twist – A True Aryan

WITH TWO WEEKS STILL TO GO before I was due to start at the German school (for Polish children) I had to embark on a series of train journeys – usually with my mother but sometimes with my father – to my father's relatives at Inowroclaw who were in dire need of help from us, especially the provision of food. This journey took five hours and involved a change of trains at Poznan.

The risks were enormous. My mother carried ration cards, obtained illegally, and the cases were filled with foodstuffs and other contraband. My father was always careful to ensure that nothing inside the cases would identify or could be traced back to us.

On these trips, my mother who spoke perfect German took an added risk by travelling in the section of the train reserved for Germans, wearing on her lapel a German Women's Association badge which she had found somewhere. My father, as a matter of principle, would not do this. He travelled with his fellow Poles in the poorer section where passengers were subjected to greater scrutiny and harassment. Entrances to the carriages were always at the front and rear and for this reason he always positioned us as near to the centre as he could manage.

Whatever section I happened to be in, I wandered up and down the corridors throughout these journeys, looking out for police or military particularly at stations during train stoppages. I had been well drilled by my father in what to observe. Two policemen climbing into a carriage was of no great concern but when an official party comprising two policemen, two uniformed SS and two plain-clothes Gestapo men (whom I could recognise easily enough) entered together, then we were in for a thorough search and scrutiny. My duty was to keep either parent informed.

On one occasion with my father, just before our train pulled out of Poznan, I saw two parties of six policemen rush down the platform. One party climbed in at the front of the Polish section and one at the back. I reported to my father immediately. He told me to go to the forward carriage of the Polish section to see what was happening while he went off towards the rear. Every compartment was being searched, every piece of baggage opened.

We met again in the corridor near our seats and I glanced anxiously at my father's two heavy cases in the rack above. He had little time to think and realised we wouldn't have time to reach the next station before the searchers arrived.

"Go," he whispered urgently, "as far forward as you can, away from the cases. Get out at the next station, cross the platform and take the first train back to Szamotuly. I'll have to jump. We'll meet again in the forest."

"What about the cases?" I asked.

"Let the Germans have them." He gave me a gentle push, pointing forward. When I glanced back I saw him disappear at the other end of the carriage.

I waited for the train to stop, paralysed with fear. Just as it slowed down I saw the police enter our carriage. I got out at the station and I was shaking but nobody seemed to notice. I had to wait three hours for the next train back to Szamotuly. I arrived home about six in the evening, cold and hungry. My father wasn't there and my mother was very anxious but there was nothing we could do. Next day around noon he arrived home, limping and bruised with a lacerated hand but otherwise fine.

A few days later I was travelling with my mother in the German section. As we changed trains at Poznan a tall friendly German took my mother's suitcase, commenting on how heavy it was. He heaved it on to the high rack opposite where my mother took her seat. She thanked him and then began to converse with an elegant lady sitting opposite and directly under the suitcase. I went out into the corridor on look-out as usual.

About half an hour later, just as the train slowed down for a station stop, my mother came out into the corridor. She beckoned to me, clearly troubled.

"We must separate and get out at the station," she told me. She parted from me before I could ask her why. I climbed out at the front end of the carriage and saw her alight at the other. I noticed she didn't have the suitcase. After the train pulled out again we got together with a two-hour wait for a train back to Poznan. Then she told me: "That man must have broken a bottle when he put the case on the rack. I noticed some oil leaking from it and running down the wall towards the lady's shoulder. But she hadn't noticed nor had anybody else. Maybe they haven't yet but I doubt that."

Another suitcase lost; neither for the first time nor the last. What became of it we would never know. The contents were all items in short supply and the Germans were short too. If they opened it they were more likely to confiscate the contents rather than report it. Sometimes they showed little conscience, or dignity, when it came to acquiring contraband.

I can recall one pathetic illustration of that.

We Poles had just about the same rights as stray dogs. We could only enter buses after all German passengers had been seated. One dark afternoon, returning home from Szamotuly, my mother managed with a couple of other Poles to get a seat on a very crowded bus. Shortly after leaving town the bus was stopped by two German civilians. Angered to find no seats available, they shouted loudly: "All Polaks out!" The Polish passengers simply had to get out.

My mother still had 5 kilometres to travel. (Some of the Poles would have up to 20 kilometres!)

She had to get home and walked on alone in the fading twilight. After about half a kilometre she became aware of a car overtaking her. She knew the driver had to be German but she raised an arm to stop the vehicle.

The driver stopped and she asked him in German for a lift. He was friendly and told her to get in. Obviously he presumed she was German too. As he drove on he asked why she was walking. There had been an accident, she told him, and the bus radiator had been damaged. It was going to take a couple of hours for the authorities to send another bus. She had to walk. She was going to Brodziszewo, she told him. When they reached the crossroads he made to turn left into the village.

"No, please, I have to go to the right, here."

"To the right?" He frowned. "But that's a Polak place down there."

"Yes. That's my husband," she explained.

His face exploded in anger. "Out!" He reached across her lap and pushed the door open.

"Machen Sie das Sie aber sofort raus kommen!" He roared and pushed her roughly so that she fell out on to the road. With the door still open he pushed the accelerator. The door smashed into the back of her head, stunning her. Scarcely conscious she watched him drive away.

At first on arrival home she said nothing. But during the evening meal she complained of a severe headache and told us what happened. She didn't know who he was but it was hardly an unusual incident. That, generally, was how the Germans treated Poles.

The really ugly twist came two days later. A car drove into our yard and a heavily built man climbed out. My father went to greet him.

"Guten Tag," the man said.

"Guten Tag," my father answered in German. I was standing just behind him.

"I'm Dr. Wagner. Your wife knows me. Two days ago I had occasion to throw her out of my car over there on the main road. She must have told you."

"She told me nothing. What can I do for you?"

The man's tone changed. He spoke quietly, almost pleadingly. "My wife badly needs a little soap. I would appreciate it if you could let me have just a piece"

"I can't do that, Doctor. Everything, up to the last piece, must be handed over to the German authorities. I can make no exceptions." My father stopped here, pondering, then he continued. "But I'll see what I can do for you."

Leaving the open-mouthed doctor standing at the gate, my father walked off to the plant section where the soap was normally cut. He reached for some grease-proof paper, then changed his mind and tore a corner piece of a German newspaper lying on the bench. Using a knife he pushed some soap scrapings mingled with dust on to the piece of paper, rolled these together in his fingers, then put the grimy ball into the piece of newspaper and returned to the waiting doctor.

"That's the best I can do for you, Herr Doctor." He handed over the pathetic morsel, then, with a curt: *"Aufwiedersehen"*, he turned his back and walked into the house.

From the window we watched the doctor drive away while my father with a bewildered expression commented: "How can a supposedly intelligent human being grovel like that. Now there's a true Aryan for you!"

🦅

Every Pole is named after a saint and every saint has a feast day. That feast day is the 'name day' of the person who carries the saint's name. My father's (Czeslaw) name day was July 20 and my mother's (Klara) was August 12. Poles like to celebrate name days not birthdays.

If my father had his way there would be no celebration of his name day. In the circumstances of the times – the dangers and the suffering that surrounded them – it seemed to him an unwarranted indulgence to celebrate his name day.

My mother thought differently. She was very gregarious and grasped at any excuse to have a party and be happy. And on this occasion she prevailed. Fortunately we had a gramophone. Without musicians, a gramophone was the only means of providing music for a celebration.

It was now illegal for Poles to possess a gramophone. An edict a year before had obliged Poles to hand in all gramophones to the authorities. Perhaps gramophones were seen to have propaganda potential. But my father had held on to ours. Living as we did on the edge of the forest, we had a better chance of getting away with this.

Good food was produced, the vodka flowed and the celebrations went on into the early hours of the morning. Around 5 am the guests began returning to their homes in Szamotuly. My father had to go into Szamotuly that day and, accompanied our friend Matusz Sylvester. They went together on their bicycles.

Matusz had wanted to borrow the gramophone, which folded into a neat wooden case. My father was happy to let him have it. In fact he insisted on carrying it for him and hung it on the handlebars of his bicycle.

As they pedalled along slowly in the morning twilight they were overtaken by another cyclist. Glancing back they noticed, since the bike frame was not, like theirs, painted white, this other cyclist must be German.

All Poles were required to salute Germans when either passed. Those wearing hats or caps were required to raise them and bring them down arms – length to their thighs. Matusz gave the German the full ritual salute. My father, never subservient, merely raised his hat a few centimetres above his crown and returned it. The German noticed.

He rode on several meters, stopped, got off, turned and signalled my father to halt. Matusz cycled on. The German rested his bike against an adjacent tree and strolled back slowly to my father. He said nothing but his eyes rested on the wooden case suspended from the handlebars. Casually he lifted this off the handlebars, feeling its weight, then abruptly slung it hard into my father's face, knocking out several teeth. Then calmly he replaced the gramophone on the handlebars while the blood spread and dripped from my father's face.

"Now, you Polak bastard, you will remember how to salute a German properly."

Matusz, who had watched all from a distance, now came back. He looked at my father's blood-covered face and started to laugh. Despite the pain my father too tried to laugh but couldn't. Matusz echoed a popular Polish cant of the time. "There, you see, the Germans cannot even win the war on a gramophone." He pointed to the wooden case on the handlebars.

"We've still got the gramophone!"

C·H·A·P·T·E·R 12

The Power Above Us

O<small>N</small> 1 S<small>EPTEMBER</small>, 1943 I <small>STARTED</small> at the German school for Polish children. This meant for me a half-hour's walk through the forest each morning to the village of Lipnica.

The first morning I arrived to find a crowd of Polish boys and girls waiting outside the school. I realised these would be the only school age Poles still left in the district.

There was nobody to greet us so we chatted away in Polish. Finally a short plump middle-aged woman emerged from a villa close to the school. This was obviously our teacher because she came across the schoolyard without any acknowledgement of our presence, opened the school door and, with a sullen expression, admitted us in to the solitary classroom.

I counted as we entered. There were 45 of us. Some knew no German whatsoever; some could speak a little. I was the only one among them fairly fluent in that language.

I disliked this woman instinctively. I could sense her animosity and had the feeling she might be very dangerous. She wore a Nazi Party badge and her voice was harsh and authoritive when she spoke. I coined a nickname for her immediately – *'Wanze'* which means bed bug. But the bed bugs at our home were never as threatening as this unpleasant woman.

Her first words were typical of what we had come to expect from the Germans. "From now on you are forbidden to speak Polish." She eyed us coldly to ensure her words were sinking in. "Not in the classroom, not in the school yard, not even at home."

This caused some of us to giggle. What she asked was impossible. We knew that this was a challenge, no matter how much she might threaten, the *'Wanze'* couldn't win. At every break during the three hours of schooling we reverted to Polish. She soon put an end to that. There would be no more breaks, just three hours of non-stop classwork!

After a few days I was dismayed to find the *'Wanze'* taking a greater interest in me than the others. She had realised I was proficient in German. On the last school day that week, after class, she told me to follow her to her villa.

It was an invitation I didn't want, concerned at what my classmates might think, but I had no option. At the villa she showed me around and told me she lived alone, her only company is the charlady who came on Saturdays. She showed me a portrait photograph of her husband in, as I could have expected, a black SS uniform. He had gone missing in the war two years earlier.

She gave me a glass of lemonade, then the questions began.

"You speak German so well. Who taught you?"

I told her simply: "My parents taught me." I could hardly tell her how it had come about.

This sparked a barrage. What do you parents do? Where do they come from? Do you have brothers or sisters? She asked if I could read or write the old (Gothic) German script. No, I couldn't.

At that she informed me that, from then on, I would return with her twice a week to the villa.

She would teach me to read and write Gothic script.

"You have good handwriting, well suited to Gothic," she told me.

A little later she informed me that she had selected me as her special student. In the future, whenever she couldn't attend classes, I was to stand in for her as teacher. As I was about to leave she said: I would like to meet your parents. This troubled me: I wondered why.

My parents wondered too when I told them during the evening meal. But we would soon find out. One afternoon two weeks later she arrived by bus at our home. My parents were cautious but courteous and offered her coffee. She asked about our family background and seemed to enjoy herself. As she was leaving she said: "I will surprise you soon with some good news."

That intrigued us without raising any great expectation. Two weeks later, after school, she called me over and said that my parents, indeed the whole family, should wait at home next afternoon for a surprise visit.

It turned out cold, wet and windy, and we watched an Opel sedan drive into our property. Two men and two women emerged, one of them the *'Wanze'*. She introduced all of us to the three state officials. One of the men commented as to how pleased the Führer would be with our family, raising four fine boys who spoke German so well.

My parents got the message: my father realized instantly what they were about. But we all waited patiently while they enlightened us. Openly they began calculating the percentage of German blood in each of us. My mother had been born in

THE AUTHOR, TED KAZMIERSKI IN 1946

Oranienburg near Berlin, so they credited her with 80 per cent. My father had been born in Inowroclaw, which, according to them, was German soil. Furthermore, he had served in the German Army in the 1914-1918 war. For this they credited him with 85 per cent. Hilary, Waldemar and I, they conceded, had inherited some German blood from our parents but Joachim, because he was born in the German Reich (occupied Poland) was also credited with 80 per cent.

After they had finished their serious calculations, although it must have been obvious they had made little impression on any of us, they continued with the charade. They handed my father an official application form for *'Volksdeutscher'* Category 3 citizenship, which meant a citizen of German descent and emphasised the great honour conferred if the application were accepted. (I glanced at the stupid *'Wanze'* and thought she thinks she's doing us a great favour.) They all stood up and the senior of the two men said they would return in a week to collect the signed application form. And, of course, he advised us, it would not be in our interest to decline. Then with due courtesy they left the house and drove away.

From that time on I hated going to school each morning and having to smile at the *'Wanze'*. Not even once at home did my parents refer to the application and I couldn't help wondering what would happen a week later when the Germans returned.

The very next day, to our great surprise and pleasure, Eberhard Hermesmann arrived on his first furlough from the Eastern Front. Next afternoon the Hermesmann family arrived at our place and Herr Hermesmann gave us the latest news from the BBC in London. Eberhard told us of great suffering and heavy losses by the German forces on the Eastern Front.

The following day Eberhard invited me to go with him to see the great German classic film: *'Der Grosse Koenig'* at the cinema in Szamotuly. When I reminded him that only Germans were permitted into the cinema for the film he told me not to worry.

"You will be accompanied by a German soldier and I still have my Hitler Youth badge at home which I can lend you."

No questions were asked as Eberhard and I entered the cinema. We had been enjoying the movie for about half an hour when suddenly the program stopped and the lights went on.

Gestapo officers and police came in and took up positions at every exit and along every fourth row.

They scrutinised the patrons. Eberhard and I chatted away and exchanged jokes in German. Little notice was taken of us. Ten minutes went by before, the scrutiny over, the Gestapo and police left without making an arrest. The program resumed.

My times with Eberhard were always exciting which is why, even today, more than 50 years on, I miss him so much. I was never able to find out what became of him or his family. He would have been only 16 when, most likely, he died at the front. The family, with their anti-Nazi leanings, may have been exterminated in the end.

Eberhard came around again next day after I got back from school. My parents had gone to Poznan so we had the house to ourselves. He related to me his different experiences as a young *'Luftwaffenhilfe'* soldier at the front. We became bored and suddenly he took up the phone book and said: "Don't worry, Ted. I want to make a call or two to upset the damned Nazis. They'll never find out who it is."

"Go ahead," I told him.

His call was to an old metalfabrik owner we knew about. With an authoritative voice he ordered a boiler to be delivered urgently to a local army unit. The old man accepted the order and promised to do all in his power to have the boiler ready for collection in five days.

Eberhard put down the phone and we shared a great laugh. He reached for the phone book again. His next call would cause a real stir but its consequences could have cost us our lives.

Identifying himself as the senior police officer responsible for air raid warnings he phoned the local *'Reichsarbeitsdienstmädchen'* (Women's Land Army) unit which we knew were working in the forest. He told them they must take cover and sound their siren to warn everyone to take shelter. They should continue to shelter until he gives them the all clear. I could hardly credit the confident way he put it across. Again we had a great laugh. Almost immediately we heard the siren, which was only a kilometre away, sounding.

Now he suggested we go over to his place and on the way we could observe if the *'Reichsarbeitsdienstmädchen'* were sheltering in the forest trenches. As we came close the girls started yelling at us to keep clear of the roadway and take cover as enemy planes were approaching.

For the next two hours at Eberhard's place we listened for the all clear which never came. On my way home I approached the trenches again to see if the girls were still there. They were empty. The girls had obviously returned to their barracks.

My parents had arrived home shortly before me. Some 10 minutes later a car drove into our yard: two uniformed SS officers and a plainclothes Gestapo official, a telephone technician as it turned out, entered the house. They tested the phone, questioned first my father and then me, ordered each of us in turn to speak over the phone. Our voices were not what they hoped to identify. They left as abruptly as they had arrived, clearly angry and frustrated.

We were the only Poles in the district to have a telephone and my parents were puzzled and concerned about the check-up. It was six months before I dared to tell them what Eberhard had done. They were not amused.

Eberhard came over again to say 'good-bye' the day before he returned to the front.

It was a sad moment for us; we liked him so much. My mother cried and hugged him as if he were her own son and we accompanied him through the forest half way back to his home. He continued on alone. It was the last time that we were ever to see him. The last sight of a very dear friend.

From the time I had started at the German school my days were fully occupied. I would leave for Lipnica at 7.30 in the morning and get home about 30 minutes after midday.

Each day brought new activities around the home and interesting news from afar.

Frequently my father went into Szamotuly where, from different sources, he would gather the latest news. This was always related to us at nightime when he came home. The Germans were now retreating on all fronts. "There will be hard battles to come," he told us more than once, "but the end of the war is in sight."

It was an especially joyful moment when he told us one night that Polish forces were now fighting with the Allies in Sicily and Italy. It turned our thoughts to his younger brother Antoni who we hoped might be with these forces. Antoni had been taken prisoner by the Red Army in September 39.

The only news we had had of him since then, from his wife Celina in Inowroclaw, that he was alive in Africa "I have a feeling inside me that he may be in Italy," my father told us.

There were so much traumas in our daily lives now that little surprised me. Inevitably one day I came home with the news from the 'Wanze' that the family should be prepared for a visit the following afternoon.

"Is she bringing the whole class with her?" was my father's sardonic response.

"No," I persisted, "the other three, to pick up the application form."

"Oh yes," my father responded. "I had forgotten all about that. Well, they can come, but don't let us bother about it."

His seeming indifference made me curious. Would it be all so simple? Why then had we been warned of the consequences if my parents failed to sign? But my father's assurance set my mind at ease and I was able to sleep well. But I heard my parents whispering in the kitchen until very late.

An hour before class ended next day the 'Wanze' called me up, she had to go to town and that I should take over the class. She showed me what to do, where the school keys were kept and where I should put them. Saying 'good-bye' she reminded me: "I'll see you in the evening."

As soon as we saw her drive away in the bus we all relaxed. We hurried through our schoolwork, breaking into Polish to communicate with each other. We were suddenly carefree.

At home in the afternoon, at the same time as the previous week, the same car with the same occupants drove into our yard. They joined us in the living room in what started like a normal afternoon's conversation. After a while the senior official with the Nazi Party badge prominent on his lapel asked my father if he had signed the application form with its oath of loyalty.

My father answered: "To be honest I haven't had time to think about it. There is so much to be done here, problems with machinery, spare parts to be found, supervision of the workers. We have to keep things moving at all costs: we can't afford to slow production."

This impressed them, my father could see, so he continued in the same vein about the management problems he was having and the difficulties that continued to crop up with machinery stalling and the right parts so difficult to find. But he appreciated this was inevitable since there was a war on.

Then the second Party official stood up and asked my father for the application form.

My father went to his desk, opened the bottom drawer, extracted a folder untouched since he had put it away a week ago, took out the form and handed it over. The German sat down again, perused the form for a few seconds, then pointed out that it had not been signed. This, he said he could understand in the circumstances. Time was so valuable. So perhaps my parents would sign now, and they would witness the signatures. He handed the forms to both my parents and a fountain pen.

There was silence in the room. And tension. My father broke this by saying he didn't see why they should change citizenship. Signing the forms wouldn't help them to work any harder for the good of the Reich. He was already doing everything possible to ensure a quick victory.

"Can I serve the Reich any better by signing these forms?"

"Yes, naturally. You must understand that the authorities can no longer agree that an industrial enterprise of this nature can continue to be run by a Polish citizen. You are aware this is the last one in Polish hands. This is now a

German enterprise and it can no longer be managed by a Pole. You signature on this application form ensures you can stay here."

"Is my signature more important than the continuation of operations at this plant?"

"That doesn't make sense. What can my signature do for production?"

"You must understand, Herr Kazmierski, we have to have your signatures."

My father got to his feet, his expression defiant. He didn't mince his words.

"Now I want you to understand me. I was born a Pole. It is my nationality and my heritage and I shall not renounce it. I regret that I must disappoint you. But if as a Pole I cannot manage this operation I will gladly hand it over to anyone willing to take on the backbreaking work involved. It is work that is draining my health and energy day after day, and causing my family sleepless nights." He walked across the room and opened the bedroom door. "Look at those walls." He pointed to the blood marks from the bed bugs. "Over a whole year, those bugs have not allowed us a proper night's sleep. And there is no insecticide available to destroy them." He continued: "Anyone who wishes can have this place. Though I wouldn't wish it on my worst enemy. And the pain of kidney stones also denies me sleep. So why should I carry on?"

The senior German spoke with resignation, as if the problem were beyond him. "Herr Kazmierski, refusal to sign the forms is tantamount to hostility to the authorities. There is no need for me to explain what that means."

At this point the 'Wanze' and her colleague turned their attention to my mother. They told her she should talk some sense into my father.

"You must bear in mind the safety and the future of your children. The Führer takes special care of German children. As *Volksdeutsche* your children will have the same privileges as all other German children in the Third Reich and you will all be able to stay together. If you choose otherwise, we cannot help you. You will be separated and worse could happen. That will depend on the authorities."

"We have come here to offer you a good future and to ensure that you can stay here. If we have to leave here without your signatures, there is no knowing what will become of you in the near future."

The two men now turned to my father again, reiterating the advantages of signing the applications. He wouldn't budge and, finally, they announced threateningly: "If you don't sign here now that will mean the death sentence for all of you... and we don't want that to happen to you."

At that moment my thoughts turned to Waldemar and the baby, Joachim, whom Stephanie was looking after in the kitchen. The forms were again thrust in front of my parents and the fountain pen proffered. The senior man bellowed one word: *"Unterschreiben!"*

My father stared unflinchingly at both men and spoke in German.

"Es tut mir leid aber das kann ich nicht machen. Ich bin als Pole geboren und werde auch als Pole Sterben." (Forgive me but I cannot do this. I was born a Pole and a Pole I'll die.)

Suddenly my mother weakened. In a thin voice she said:

"If I sign, can you guarantee I can keep the children with me?"

"No, you cannot!" It was the second man who spoke. "We must have your husband's signature."

All four Germans stood now, obviously annoyed that they had failed in their mission.

They walked towards the door and the senior man turned again towards my parents.

"You will get one more chance to sign. Another 24 hours. At this time tomorrow somebody else will come to collect the signed forms. If you still refuse, well, I don't have to explain what you can expect."

My father accompanied them out to the car and said 'good-bye'. He closed the gate behind them and returned to the house casually as if nothing that happened.

He sat at his desk and gathered some papers and put them in a drawer. Stephanie brought Waldemar and Joachim into the room and my mother took them onto her lap. Hilary and I went over to our father at his desk. "What will happen tomorrow?" we asked him.

At first he didn't reply. After a while he reached out and took our hands in his. He explained why he could not sign. His conscience would not allow him.

"To accept such degradation and humiliation by signing those papers while millions of Poles are dying at the hands of the Germans is something beyond me. We have to be very strong in our beliefs now and remember we should never renounce who we are for the benefit of the enemy."

"We don't have the power to oppose the Germans. But there is a power above who will watch over us and allow us to stay here. God is testing us with this ordeal. Every day for us here means danger. Tomorrow will be no different from any other day. We have to be prepared for trials even greater than this. There is nothing else we can do. But if we manage to stay here we must work harder than ever to help others."

Next morning, like every other morning, I went to school. The 'Wanze's' attitude had changed. She treated me now with total indifference. I was expecting this and some-how was prepared for it. Every lesson, every hour seemed an eternity. Today might be my last day here. I had only one desire – to get home quickly and be with my parents and brothers, and wondering if they would still be there. I took a short cut through the forest. Normally I would have walked leisurely, enjoying all the wonders of nature which it offered. But not today. I just hurried.

When I arrived my father was busy in the yard. In the living room my mother was making a parcel. Nothing had changed. At the dinner table there was total silence. My father never spoke much during meals but my mother was always chattering. Not today however. There was just fore-boding as the day wore on. Nobody came. Even the phone failed to ring.

As night approached our anxiety increased. My father hid his emotions but was aware, as much as the rest of us, that about 6 o'clock the 24 hours would be up. We didn't know what was to come.

The next few days came and went, each one easing the pressure of our anxiety. But nothing further happened. And never did.

C·H·A·P·T·E·R 13

My Mother at the Gestapo Headquarters

This was a time when, as each day passed, we had little time to reflect, ever preoccupied with what the next day would bring and wondering when we might be removed from the forest.

Over the past year or two I had observed that, whenever my father was pressurised by German threats, he would work harder and faster in his efforts to help the oppressed people in the countryside around us.

When I asked him once how much longer he would continue in these efforts, so fraught with danger for all of us, his answer was: "So long as we are here and God gives us the chance to help people in need, we must continue to do so. There is no other way. In another year or two the war will be over and then we can relax and thank God for sparing us. But for now we must push on and have faith and then nothing will fail."

I was about to ask him how he could be sure that God would continue to protect us when he interrupted by telling me that tomorrow after school I was to go to Szamotuly and deliver two small parcels to an important German person whom I had never met. "In return he will give you an envelope which you must bring back to me." He added that, the day after, I would have to go with my mother to Inowroclaw and I had to find an excuse to be absent from school for two days.

He always insisted that I walk to school, because the other Polish children did not have bikes and I should do as they did. "Besides," he went on, breaking into a sarcastic smile, "The bike must always be ready for the factory needs – so we can work toward victory for the German Reich."

Next day after lunch, (our main meal which was always served around one o'clock when I had arrived from school) I got out my bicycle and got ready to ride to Szamotuly. My father handed me two parcels, each marked in heavy black ink: 'For the Eastern Front.' His instruction was precise and clear. If I were stopped and confronted with any risk or danger I should proceed by bringing them direct to the Post Office for posting. Otherwise I was to deliver them to a new block of units in Ostroroska Street. He gave me the unit number and said: "The man you will deliver them to is a high ranking S.A. (Brown Shirts) officer, so don't be shocked if he is in uniform when he opens the door. He will be expecting you. Leave the push-bike some distance away, at least 100 metres, and walk to the unit through the back entrance."

As I left my father asked me to make the Sign of the Cross and warned my to be very careful on the way back and not to allow myself to be accosted by the Germans.

I left for Szamotuly, happy to be on my bike again. As I got near the town it started to rain, at first a fine shower but gradually it got heavy. On the cobblestones of the inner streets it was difficult to ride the bike and avoid the puddes.

Although it was prohibited, as there was nobody in sight I took the chance, rode up on to the footpath and continued. I was riding on the footpath for no more than two minutes when suddenly, from a house entrance ahead of me a policeman emerged. He called on me to halt. It was still raining heavily and now I was worried about the parcels. Fortunately he wasn't interested in them but demanded: "You know it is forbidden to ride on the footpath?"

"Yes, I know," I answered guiltily.

At that he strode up to me and, with the full force of his open palm, struck me across the face, so that I fell heavily to the ground, still astride the bicycle.

"Now in future, you Polak," he yelled out, "you will remember". Then he strode back into the house.

I was hurt. There was flashing in my temples and a drum beating in my ears. Slowly I hauled myself to my feet, took the bike back on to the street and climbed on. I had still two kilometres to go.

The address I had was on the other side of the town. I found it easily enough, carefully following my father's instructions. It was the S.A. man's wife who opened the door and, in a friendly tone, invited me in. I felt awkward and uncomfortable in my wet clothes. She invited me into the living room, took the parcels (which I presumed contained soap) and handed them to her husband who was sitting in an armchair in his brown uniform and reading a newspaper, which he put aside. He welcomed me and told his wife to make me coffee and warm me up.

I sensed that he could see something had happened to me and tried to hide the hurt side of my face from him. The flat, I noticed, was cosy: these people were used to a comfortable lifestyle. When I finished my 'ersatz' coffee, he gave me a thick envelope, telling me to be careful and not lose it. In the passageway I put the envelope in a special bag my mother had sewn for me and tied to my waist, hidden under my shirt. I had no idea what the envelope contained.

It was still raining, and windy as I left the block of units, a typical autumn day in Poland.

I decided to ride home by a different route – somewhat longer but safer. I had scarcely travelled two kilometres when, in the distance, I could see a gang of young Germans, obviously Hitler Youth, and that meant real trouble. This was a familiar situation to me: they were waiting to ambush any Poles who might pass, and beat them up.

I retraced my steps and took again the route I had come by earlier. About 30 minutes later I arrived at a corner at Galowo on the other side of town which my mother had often warned me about – where the police and the Hitler Youth liked to wait to trap Poles. I felt anxious now knowing that I was carrying with me something contraband. I got off my bike and climbed into a field to get a view around the corner without being seen. Sure enough there they were! In fact a large contingent.

I could not proceed. I knew they couldn't see me so I decided to wait, hidden in the field. An hour later they were still there and I was wet, cold and miserable. I couldn't go deeper into the wet muddy field, so I decided to return to Szamotuly.

Darkness was falling, my shoes were mud-covered and I had a dreadful headache from the blow received earlier. In this condition I didn't want anybody to see me. So what to do?

I had to get home because tomorrow I had to accompany my mother to Inowroclaw.

I decided to ride to the Coal Storage Depot where a Polish driver I knew I could trust was working. Just as I arrived I saw him some distance inside. He looked as if he were about to go home.

I waited until he arrived at the gate. He didn't recognise me but I explained who I was and told him I needed to get back to the 'forest' tonight and that I must not be caught by the Germans. He said that this afternoon the police and the Hitler Youth were active on every main road stopping people.

"Don't worry," he said. "I'll get you home safely. But not now. The are still Germans in the office and on the gate. After six o'clock there will be Poles on duty. I'll go back then and get a truck. Be at the gate at six."

For the next hour I took shelter in the local railway station nearby. At six o'clock I returned and met him near the gate. He told me to wait and went to collect the truck about 100 metres away. When he reached me he got out and put my bike in the back of the truck, which had high sides. He told me it would be safer for me to get in the back also and crouch down in case he was stopped. There was still some coal in the truck, which blackened my clothes. As we went by the bend at Galowo I peered out. The police and Hitler Youth were still there. They didn't stop him. He drove on a couple of kilometres, then stopped and dropped me off with the bicycle and turned back. I continued on home.

My mother was shocked at the state I was in, black from the coal. I gave the big envelope to my father and got ready to wash and change. Later I asked him what was in the envelope. "Ration cards," he told me, "for food and clothes. Tomorrow, with your Mum, you'll be taking them to Inowroclaw."

When I awoke early next morning the left side of my face was bruised and swollen.

My parents decided I should stay at home: my mother would go to Inowroclaw on her own.

She packed a large suitcase with pork fat, lard and other foodstuffs. She took a handful of the *Kleiderkarten* (clothing ration cards) which I had brought home last evening and put them into her handbag and my father drove her to the train. He returned in about two hours and said my mother would be back next day but I always worried about her on these trips.

About 11 o'clock the phone rang. I picked up the receiver. A man, speaking in Polish, asked for my father. "It is urgent," he said. I realised it was not a local call, so hurried out to call my father.

Listening to my father's part of the conversation I know that whatever the news was it wasn't good. As soon as my father put down the phone I asked him who the man was and what had happened.

My father didn't reply straight away. Instead he stood pondering in silence for several seconds, and then he drew me to his side and spoke in a calm composed voice.

"That man is one of many who know us and, I am sure, is aware of our illegal activity. He saw Mum getting into the German section of the train at Szamotuly and went on to the Polish section. He saw Mum again as she got out at Poznan to change trains and observed that a man was following her. He decided to keep an eye on them both. There was a railway policeman at the checkpoint and as Mum presented her ticket the man following her told the policeman he should arrest Mum, that she had picked up something from English POWs. He saw Mum put down the suitcase before she searched for her ticket. He quickly picked up the suitcase as if it were his own, nodded to Mum and passed through. He saw the policeman take Mum away and took her suitcase to the left luggage office and got a docket for it. He would wait for Mum outside the police station and give her the docket when she comes out."

"All we can do now is wait till Mum phones us." He finished speaking and I could see from his expression that he was very worried. A minute or two later I was asking questions again.

"Did the man make any mention of the 'Kleiderkarten'?"

"No."

"Then what will happen if the police find them?"

"If that happens it will be dreadful for her... and for all of us. So don't think about it. Instead just pray to God that they will find nothing and let her go. We can do nothing more now except trust in God."

Hours passed. My father tried to keep busy outside. I stayed close to the phone waiting anxiously for Mum's call. But no call came.

The time dragged on slowly. Even outside in the yard there was little activity. I could hear nothing except the steady regular beat from the engine and press in the plant. Another hour passed and then the phone rang.

"That's Mum," I called out excitedly and picked it up. No, not Mum, but the same voice that had spoken to me earlier, again asking for my father urgently.

My father had just arrived in the room, in response to the phone ringing. He took the receiver from my hand. I waited, impatient to learn some news of Mum. As soon as he put down the receiver I blurted out: "What happened to Mum?"

My father tried to be calm and spoke in a reasoned tone. "That poor man has spend hours watching the railway police station. He says he has seen Mum being escorted out by an armed policeman and taken to the Gestapo headquarters. That was all he could do – and I'm thankful for what he has done. I have told him to pick up the suitcase and keep the contents or share them with his family and friends."

He hung his head and drew me again to his side. There were tears in his eyes. He was silent and I sensed that he was thinking of the same thing that I was, something he had told me a little time ago, that whoever is taken into the Gestapo Headquarters never comes out. For Poles there is only one way – into the building. There is no way out alive – except to prison and execution or the concentration camp.

It was a sad tearful afternoon for all of us after this grave news. We couldn't stop thinking about what Mum would be going through. I wanted to ask my father countless questions. I knew that since Mum had been arrested they would soon pick up the rest of us. I could see our situation was helpless: there was nothing my father could do.

I was crying and my father tried to console me, tried to assure me that everything would be all right and that soon Mum would be back with us. I had a feeling that he wanted to be left alone. He was the only one that in such situations never showed weakness. I also knew that he had always been right when he said that God would protect us. But this time I had doubts: I could not believe him. So I went outside to leave father alone.

I couldn't stay in the yard weeping and let everybody see me with tears in my eyes. So I went deep into the forest and sat on a bench I had myself erected there. Here the world seemed different and peaceful. In this part of the forest the autumn is beautiful but it also looks as if everything is dying.

There I started to pray to God that Mum would be released from the Gestapo. But my thoughts kept wandering. I couldn't finish even one simple short prayer. I tried again and again. It was easy for my father to say to me that the only thing we could do was to pray – even when the situation was hopeless; that God would be listening. I wanted to believe him but after all I had seen – how this 'Herrenvolk' loved to kill with such great satisfaction defenceless, helpless people, why they would now spare Mum.

They didn't have to answer, or take any responsibility, for what they were doing, and I know that we are not the first, and would not be the last to suffer at their hands. Suddenly a feeling of great indifference came over me. I decided to return home.

Walking into our yard I looked for my father. He wasn't around. I couldn't find him in the living room either, where he was often sitting at his desk. I went to the machinery room and he wasn't there, so I began to worry. I found Marie and asked if she had seen him.

"He's in the bedroom. He doesn't want to be disturbed," she told me. But I had to find out what he was doing. Was he unwell? Has he gone to bed? Quietly, without making a noise, I opened the bedroom door a little.

He was down on his knees beside the bed, praying before the big picture of Jesus on the Hill of Olives, the picture that forever seemed to dominate the bedroom. He was praying in a low voice. Slowly I closed the door, went away and sat at my father's desk, picked up the framed portrait of Adolf Hitler, turned it over and studied the picture of Mum. I couldn't stop looking at her; focussing on her and conscious of a gleam of hope that something good was going to happen. The hope grew.

I heard my father come into the room from the bedroom. His hand fell on my shoulder.

In silence together we both studied Mum's picture. After a while he spoke quietly: "Ted, I'm convinced that Mum will be with us soon again." But I felt he was saying this just to console me, to assure me that everything would be all right. He gestured to me to come with him and we went outside into the yard. There his mood changed.

We both brightened and began to feel optimistic. But a few hours later as we all sat inside at the table to start our evening meal the gloomy atmosphere returned. We were all ominously conscious of Mum's empty chair. My father said grace and added an extra prayer, after which a deep and anxious silence fell over us. We went through the motions of eating but were all preoccupied with thoughts of Mum. The only sound to break the silence was Marie tending to the baby Joachim and Waldemar. She put Joachim to bed and prepared to feed Waldemar.

The depression continued to hang over us until the end of the meal when my father suggested: "Come, let's go outside to the garden and sit on the bench." Resignedly we went with him.

In the quiet outside we could hear the passing traffic 200 metres away on the main road.

Gradually this lessened as twilight slowly gave way to darkness. From time to time we could hear the occasional motor vehicle approaching and passing. At each approach I would have the feeling; this is it; they're coming now for the rest of us. Only my father remained composed and confident. We listened to the wind whistling through the trees that reached for over 40 metres into the dark sky, the cooing of owls in the depths of the forest and a variety of birdsong farewelling the passing daylight.

There was an increasing cacophony from croaking frogs and far off we could hear the rattle of trains approaching and departing Szamotuly, seven kilometres away.

Suddenly the phone rang. My father jumped from the bench and hurried into the house to answer it. Hilary and I went across to the open window to listen to the conversation.

The first word we heard him utter was 'Mamulka'. We knew, with a feeling of hope and joy that Mother was on the other end. Mostly our father was listening before he put down the receiver. He came out and the expression on his face told us what we so much wanted to know even before he spoke. "Mum is at the station at Szamotuly. I have to go now and pick her up. Everything is okay." He hurried away to the yard to get the Citroën truck.

After he had left Hilary and I sat in the garden discussing how it was that Mum had been released from the Gestapo. That just did not happen to Poles. And even more puzzling to us, how she had come to be arrested in the first place. Well, we would soon know.

Shortly before 10 o'clock, just at curfew, we heard the Citroën turning off the main road towards the house. We rushed to meet them at the gate. Mother did not want to go inside yet, but came instead and sat on the garden bench in the darkness. We felt she was too tired to tell us everything but shortly she told us she had been arrested for picking up a small can of condensed milk thrown into the carriage from a train carrying British POWs just as the train pulled into Poznan station. It was for this reason that she was taken into custody. She assured us that everything was now fine but she wanted us to go to bed and in the morning she would tell us everything. She kissed us both and told us to say our prayers. Father would not come with us as he always did because Mum had many things she wanted to talk over with him.

At our bedside, with much relief, Hilary and I knelt down and thanked God for bringing Mum safely back to us. But infected with all the excitement of that day and anxiety for the next day when she promised to tell us everything, it was many hours before Hilary or I could fall asleep.

I was up very early next morning, long even before Mother was up, and that was unusual, especially as I still had a day off from school, arranged because of my swollen face. It was quite a while later when my mother came slowly into the living room and when we saw her, Hilary and I was shocked. I knew then why she had stayed out in the garden and sent us off to bed before we could see her in the light. This was not the Mum we knew, always busy and efficient and forever smiling. Her face was blotched red and blue from bruising, looking as if she had fallen from a train or down steps. From her slow constrained movements it was obvious that every part of her body was hurting. We couldn't find the courage to ask her what had happened. As we sat down to breakfast she told us that, since yesterday morning, she had had nothing to eat. And yet, even now, she was unable to eat; she would only have coffee.

After the rest of us had finished, and before Maria began to clear the table, she finally took a few morsels. Then she told us her story.

"As the train pulled into the station at Poznan somebody lowered the carriage window. There was a train stationery on the tracks beside us with English POWs. They began to throw cans at the open windows across into our train, and a can of condensed milk landed at my feet. I picked it up and put it in my handbag. A middle-aged German civilian sitting opposite told me I was breaking the law. Who cares, I thought. I ignored him. As I left the train I realised I would have an hour's wait for the train to Inowroclaw, and I became conscious that the German civilian who had spoken was following close behind. Whenever I stopped he stopped, determined to stay behind me. So I decided to get out of the station. As I reached the checkout I put down the suitcase to get out my ticket. At that moment the German crossed my path and spoke to the railway policeman standing beside the checkout.

"Arrest this lady. She has picked up some present from the English POWs."

Just then a man I didn't know gave me a look of recognition and picked up my suitcase as if it were his own. I knew he must be a friend, not a thief, and felt relieved. The contents of the case could have meant big trouble for me.

"My ticket was punched and the policeman ordered me to go with him. I just managed to remove the little badge of the German Women's League from my lapel and conceal it. I still had the ration cards in my handbag and knew if I couldn't get rid of them quickly it would mean the end for me. But there was no opportunity. The Police Headquarters were in the same building as the Railway Administration. On entering I was confronted by a policeman behind a desk who began to fill in a form, throwing questions at me regarding my name, my address, the purpose of my train journey and so on."

"After this I was moved roughly into another room where a lone police officer sat behind a desk. He started by asking me why I had picked up the can, then ordered me to empty the contents of my pockets and handbag, all my possessions, and put them on the desk in front of him. As I fetched out the envelope from the handbag and put it with the rest of the items on the table I was trembling. Meticulously he examined every item, taking his time, until only the thick envelope remained. This he touched with the back of his fingers, somewhat indifferently, looked at me and stood up. He walked to the door and opened it, ordering me to gather up everything and go with him."

"Scarcely able to believe my luck, if that was what it was, I collected all my possessions and returned them to my handbag and pockets and went with him."

(Listening to Mum at this stage of her story I was reminded of my father's words on another occasion: "The Lord who made the blind see can make the sighted blind.")

"They led me into another room where four or five police officers were preoccupied with deskwork. One of them pointed to a bench and ordered: 'Sit there and wait!' In a short time an elderly policeman, with a rifle hung from a strap over his shoulder, arrived and stood in front of me. He ordered me to accompany him, led the way out into the street and, on the footpath ordered me to walk in front of him. In silence I began to walk. Then a few minutes later I heard him ask if I could speak German and I told him I could, then enquired: 'Where are you taking me?'"

"To the Gestapo Headquarters." I felt a stab of fear. That place was about one kilometre away, a grim and foreboding building. I walked on. We were about half way there when I heard his voice again behind me speaking quietly. "Do you have anything in your possession that can cause you trouble in there. Because if you have get rid of it. Dispose of it into the next garbage bin. I will tell you when." I was confused and uplifted but could hardly believe what I was hearing. I could see a garbage bin ahead and, as we came close, I reached into my handbag and my fingers gripped the envelope with the ration cards. He was about two metres behind me and the garbage bin was beside me.

"Jetzt!" (Now!) I heard him say and out of the corner of my eye I saw him turn away, as if surveying the street scene around us. I dropped the envelope into the garbage bin and, for the moment at least, enjoyed a feeling of immense relief.

"Danke schön," I said quietly back to him. It was the only acknowledgement I could make and it seemed so inadequate. Now there would be nothing to condemn me when we reached the Gestapo Headquarters."

"Nevertheless when we entered the building I was shaking with fear. All too well I knew its reputation. He handed over the form with my particulars that had been filled in along with the can of condensed milk to an unsmiling black uniformed young man and departed."

"Alone, surrounded by black uniforms, I was pushed from one room to another. Time and again I was asked the same questions. Why had I done it? Did I not know the regulations?"

"It seemed the interrogations would never cease. Then several Gestapo officers gathered around me as I crouched on a chair and, with their open hands began to strike me across the face. Each blow brought pain, then flashes of pain, then throbbing headache until finally under the continuing rain of blows I tumbled forward on to the ground. As I lay there, trying to curl up for protection, they began to kick me with their jackboots, kicks aimed to straighten me out, so that, unprotected, their continued kicking became more damaging. Their cruel toecaps dug deep into every part of my body while I could hear them laugh and jibe. I lost consciousness."

When I came to, I was lying on the cold floor of a cellar in total darkness, every part of my body racked with pain. I don't know how long I lay there but suddenly the door opened and I was called out. Painfully I climbed to my feet and staggered to the door. The man confronting me was heavily built, black uniformed and jackbooted. Roughly he dragged me to the entrance, gave me my handbag and pushed me out on to the street. His voice followed me out. "Be warned, Polacke, never again do such a stupid thing."

"For all the pain I was filled with relief. I could not believe they had let me go. I had difficulty finding my way back to the railway station, dizzy and all my muscles and joints sore from the beating, wanting only to get back to Szamotuly."

She looked at each of us and, for the first time, there was a smile on her face.

"Anyway, I'm back home now and everything is back to normal again. And I have all of you to thank because I know you have all been praying hard for me."

Next day, Saturday, all our close friends arrived to celebrate Mother's safe return. But the trauma of her ordeal was to remain with her for a long time to come.

C·H·A·P·T·E·R 14

No Pride – The Hallmark of Vermin

THE NIGHTS BECAME LONGER as the autumn of 1943 crept by. About 10 o'clock each night Szymon would release the last shift of the St. Bernard watchdogs. Often now the dogs on this shift, as soon as they began to move freely around the yard, would break into a low whining chorus akin to the sound of evil spirits carried from afar on the winds. At this we would wander out into the yard and we could hear the rumbling of distant explosions. This told us a concentrated bombardment of some part of Germany was in progress, perhaps as far as 200 kilometres away. This nightly air bombardment became more and more frequent.

The regular visits of Herr Doctor Von Der Ouwe, the district veterinarian, became more frequent then before. His usual procedure now was, first, to spend some time outside in the yard in deep discussion with my father. What they were discussing we had no idea but it was obvious they had an unusual rapport. Then, before leaving, the good Doctor would come into the house for a cup of coffee or tea and a pleasant chat with mother and the rest of us. Despite his insignia and his usual serious expression we always had a good feeling when he visited, a feeling of security.

One afternoon in the beginning of December Dr. Von Der Ouwe arrived in his sedan. My father had been expecting him and had the Citroën truck with one of our workers out on the road waiting for him. I knew they were going somewhere with him and I asked my father if I could come too. My father gave me the nod and soon I was sitting in the cabin of the truck between my father and the worker, following the veterinary sedan. Some 20 minutes later, we arrived at a huge pig farm.

Dr. Von Der Ouwe climbed out of his car and went into the administration building. A couple of minutes later he emerged with another man and signalled us to follow him. We were soon inside the entrance of a massive pigsty. The doctor went forward and methodically examined about 50 pigs. About half of these he marked with a blue marker which indicated they carried some infectious disease and had to be destroyed immediately. Then he left.

While we waited outside the other man killed the pigs, then loaded the fresh carcasses on to the truck and we drove straight home. Nothing was said but I knew from what my father had once told me that these carcasses carried no infection. What Dr. Von Der Ouwe was doing was done at great risk. It could have cost him his life.

Over the following two nights my father, mother and Marie worked very hard into the early hours, preparing parcels of meat, pork fat and lard. Every parcel, big and small, was packed in strong grease-proof paper. My father was an expert at parcelling, methodical and fast. I would watch fascinated by his repetitive precision. Then all the parcels had to be carried up into the loft.

Next day the weather was very cold with snow expected. All day my father was busy again preparing and parcelling bars of soap. I put several questions to him but got little response. I realised he didn't like it when I asked him: 'where will all this go?' He stopped and told me that for security reason the less I knew the better. However he did say that some people would be coming that night to pick up the parcels.

After we had finished supper that evening mother started to set the table again, saying that we were expecting some Germans. Around 10 o'clock we heard the sound of a truck turning from the road towards our property. My father immediately hurried outside and I heard him tell Szymon to get the dogs under control. Then, from the window, I watched my father open the gate and let the truck in. He closed the gate behind it.

Minutes later my blood turned cold as two SS officers came with my father into the warm living room. I was prepared for a visit from some German civilians but not two like these in the black uniforms with swastika and 'Totenkopf' (skull) insignia. I was confused and concerned.

They sat at the table and mum served them snacks and vodka while my father took Hilary and Marie with him to help him load the truck outside with the parcels that had been taken down from the loft.

I observed the two SS men as they ate. They seemed intelligent and courteous enough and had removed their somewhat elegant gloves from their hands and placed them on the table. But as they consumed more vodka their mood changed: they became jovial and talkative. One of them picked up his gloves, inviting Mum and me to admire their fine texture, commenting on how fine was the skin of Polish woman from which the gloves had been made! A cold shiver coursed through my body rendering me speechless. I pulled away not knowing what to say.

They laughed and joked and tried further to get me to put on the gloves. I would only hold them in my hand, affronted by their softness, which left me in no doubt that they had indeed been made from human skin.

It was after midnight when they left. They thanked my parents profusely for the soap, which their wives would greatly appreciate. They assured us that all the food would be distributed to the hungry prisoners in time for them to have a better Christmas.

As they drove away from our yard the snow was falling heavily which pleased my father who said to my mother: "That is fortunate. It will soon conceal the tyre marks on the road and nobody will know that truck has been here."

I got ready for bed but could not sleep until my father arrived in the room. "Who were those terrible men?" I asked him. "Where were they from?"

His answer was brief and firm. "Ted, it is better to forget what they showed you and everything they said. They are vermin, human sadists, from the big prison at Wronki. But I have been assured by Dr. Von Der Ouwe that they can be relied on to distribute the food to the poor prisoners which may help them survive a little longer, and for that they were given the soap which is as valuable as gold to them. Maybe later on they will be involved in the killing of the prisoners. That is something over which I have no control. But for now they will be reliable and responsible, because of their discipline, even if under their skins they are nothing but degenerate men."

Next morning my father was the first to get up. He was already preparing more food parcels when suddenly a German police car turned into our roadway and stopped.

The policemen got out and began to examine the surface of the road.

"Quick," my father told us. "Get up and get dressed." He was aware that from the beginning of December all German farmers in the locality had been ordered to patrol the roads in four-hour shifts, over sections of one to two kilometres. These patrols worked from 10 o'clock in the evenings to six in the mornings. It was quite possible that one of these patrols had seen the truck leaving our premises and reported it to the police.

A few minutes later the police car drove up to our property and stopped at the gate. My father did not wait for them to come in; he went out to them. Sure enough, they told him that one of the road patrols had reported seeing a truck leave our premises during the night.

"Yes, yes," my father told them. "They were SS soldiers. Their truck broke down. I went out to help them."

Mention of the SS was enough, as my shrewd father well knew. Investigation of the elite SS was a taboo which not even the police dared breach. *"Danke schön."* They saluted and returned to the car. *"Aufwiedersehen!"* They drove away.

My father came back inside and immediately returned to the parcels. I could hear Mum in the kitchen and guessed she was preparing more food for the parcels. He called her to help him, as he needed to have a lot more ready to take away with him later in the day.

Mother came out of the kitchen, her arms laden, and suddenly, almost deliberately, she dropped everything. She looked exhausted, then went over to the table and pushed everything off it on to the ground. I was stunned. She was moving like a robot. She went to father's desk and pushed everything of that on to the floor. We could see she was breaking down. My father rushed over to her, tried to calm her but it was useless. She screamed, she shouted, she cried, calling out she had had enough. "I cannot stand the strain any longer. I cannot stand the strain."

We had never seen her like this before and I was shocked. Luckily there were no Germans around to hear her. After a while she quietened down. My father took her in his arms and gently laid her down on the sofa. "She's been working all through the night," he said, as if by way of explanation. Very quickly she fell asleep.

C·H·A·P·T·E·R 15

The Plant is on Fire
"We Cannot Stop Doing what we are Doing"

THIS WAS NOW THE FOURTH WINTER of the war and it started mildly. We hoped it would continue that way. There were some light frosts and good falls of snow but the temperature did not fall below minus 10 degrees centigrade. Gradually the forest settled under a lavish white fleece.

One day, totally unexpected, several members of the German Security Police (SD) arrived at our home. Without invitation they came into the living room and asked to see all of the family. The senior officer informed us that guerillas, partisans and bandits had recently become very active in this area of the forest. It was more than likely that before long some of these would come on to our property looking for food and drink. He warned us that if we spotted any of them we must inform the police immediately. "If anyone should come knocking on your door or windows at night, you must immediately, and without responding to the knock, get on the phone to the police and inform them. To give help of any kind to one of these partisans will be tantamount to signing your death warrants. *Ist das klar?*" he bellowed in conclusion.

It was clear indeed. All too clear. We nodded without speaking. Abruptly they turned and departed, my father accompanying them to the gate.

As soon as he returned to the room we gathered around him eager with questions. He quickly spelt out what he expected us to do. "If any of these people come, and we know they are partisans, we must never betray them whatever the cost. But we have a dilemma if a knock comes to the window at night and we don't know who is there. It may well be the Germans, in the guise of partisans, coming to try us out. We can only be vigilant and trust in God to see us through this because the signs are there now that this war will soon be coming to an end."

Just a few days after this I was making my way through the forest in the morning darkness on my way to school when suddenly there loomed in front of me what looked like a human shape. I could not be sure, depending on the radiance from the snow for the scant visibility. I halted for a moment, then took a few steps forward and reached out towards the shape. As I touched it I realised it was only a juniper shrub covered in snow. I started to laugh. The forest around me abounded in junipers. But I wondered how I could have made such a mistake being as familiar with the forest as I was.

The story caused laughter all around the dinner table in the early afternoon. But my father took a serious view and suggested the incident could have been a warning.

"Ted," he advised, "if I were you I would take the long route by the road to school and avoid the forest. But knowing you I am sure you will still persist in going through the forest because you feel safe and at home there." He was right, of course.

Only two days later, going through the forest again in the morning darkness and no more than 500 metres from our home, I was once again confronted by the ghostly outline of what seemed a human figure. I hesitated, then decided it was again a juniper shrub. I went forward... and the shrub moved. A positive movement, I had no doubt.

"Who is there?" I whispered urgently in Polish. "Who is there?"

An answer came, clear in the darkness. "Are you Polish?"

"Yes. I am." The figure came closer. It was a man covered in a loose white cloak. He spoke first in hesitant broken Polish, then in fluent German. He asked where I had come from and where I was going. Then he asked me to describe to him exactly where he was. I tried to do this then inter-rupted myself to ask him where he had come from and what he was doing in this part of the forest. He had come from England: he had been dropped by parachute, lost contact with his colleagues and landed in a field not far from the forest.

I was filled with joy to find I was speaking with a friend from far off, an ally. It was my first experience of this kind. He asked a few more questions and I tried to help him but there was little more I could do. He had his own way to go. I shook his hand and said good-bye and carried on to school, knowing I must not mention this meeting to anybody there.

When I returned home in the early afternoon my father was not there. When he returned in the evening he brought news that the previous night in the Wronki forest region, about 20 kilometres away, a large contingent of British and Polish paratroopers had been dropped and he presumed they had joined up with the partisans.

As more and more parachutists were dropped by night, partisan activity increased in the Wronki area. At the same time, as a result of the deteriorating war situation, there was a noticeable slackening of German military regimentation. Among the Poles a new-born optimism emerged. What did it all portend? Was the end in sight for the Great German Reich which Hitler had promised would last for a thousand years. It was hardly surprising that my ever gregarious mother, sharing this sense of change, and, after all the terror and trauma she had experienced, now wanted to have a party to welcome the new year, 1944. She said nothing to my father. Early on New Year's Eve he left for Szamotuly in the horse-wagon saying we could expect him back around seven o'clock.

As soon as he had gone, she called on us to help her and began clearing away the furniture from the centre of the living room back towards the walls. Then she began to put up decorations, predominantly colourful paper lanterns which strangely, in a time of widespread shortages, always seemed to be available in the shops for celebrations. She was determined to have her New Year party.

My father would not have approved. He was aware that farmers and German farm workers had been conscripted into a force of guards that more and more were patroling the roads at night to counter the partisans. But carried along on her impulses Mum was on the phone many times to our closest friends inviting them to come and join us at eight in the evening.

About four in the afternoon all our plant workers were allowed off early because of the holiday. Then a little later we were surprised to hear Szymon shouting towards the house from the yard. We looked out and saw him heading down to the gate to open it for my father in the wagon.

Szymon unharnessed the horse and led it away and I was puzzled to see my father still sitting in the wagon. I went out to greet him. He was fast asleep. I reached up and tugged at him. Slowly he opened his eyes, looked at me and said: "Ted. I'm so tired. I just want to lie down." As he climbed down unsteadily from the wagon I could smell alcohol and was shocked to realise he was drunk. I had never seen him before in such a state and helped him into the house. In the dull interior he did not seem to notice the changes mother had made for the party. We helped him out of his overcoat, jacket and boots and laid him down on the couch.

Mother looked relieved. "Let him sleep," she said and returned to her preparations for the party. "He'll be all right by 8 o'clock."

About 15 minutes later we heard what sounded like heavy motor vehicles crunching to a halt outside our gate. We could hear the sound of voices and then came a distinctive knocking on our wicker gate. Mother quickly put a quilt over my father to conceal him from these unexpected visitors, then she and I put on our heavy coats and went outside. What we saw staggered us. Three heavy military transports had pulled up behind a jeep and dozens of Wehrmacht troops were jumping down from the transports. Two officers, obviously from the jeep, were standing outside the wicker gate and mother went over and opened it. They told us they wished to take the transports inside and mother instructed Szymon, who was standing near-by, to open the main gate.

The transports drove in and the soldiers came in behind them. They all seemed to be in an easygoing, almost jovial mood and we sensed they were not going to mean any problem for us. One officer ordered the men into marching formation and led them out again where they headed off towards the forest.

The other officer, the more senior, asked if he could use the telephone and said they wished to use our yard as field headquarters for a little time. We knew then they had not come for us and felt an enormous relief.

Mother had no choice but to invite him into our living room despite my father's condition. As he entered his eyes brightened, looking at all the colourful lanterns. He was young and we saw a look that might have been expectation, or nostalgia in his eyes, recognising, perhaps after a long absence, a real home environment. He turned to mother and said: "How much I wish I were at home tonight too... but maybe soon the war will be over." He went over to the telephone and picked it up.

As we listened to his conversation we heard him report that there were partisans operating in the forest around us. While he continued my father stirred visibly under the quilt on the couch and began to mumble. Mother tried to keep him quiet but the officer noticed. He put down the phone. Mother explained to him that her husband was sick with a fever. Not to spoil the evening she was trying to organise a party for the children. Clearly he did not disapprove but our worry was how long he might remain in the house. In less than three hours our guests would start arriving.

Around seven o'clock we could hear the soldiers returning from the forest. The officer who had gone with them came into the house and reported to the other that they had found no trace of partisans and were ready to leave. Courteously they thanked my mother and left. It was obvious they thought we were German. Minutes later we heard the heavy transports drive off and at long last were able to relax.

My father removed the quilt and sat up, confused. He wondered if he had been dreaming. Now we felt we had another reason to celebrate and looked forward to the party.

We weren't disappointed. It turned out a great party for us and the guests, some of whom stayed overnight and left shortly after daybreak.

❧

One question dominated all of our minds when the New Year arrived, would 1944 turn out to be the last year of the war. Other questions followed on. Would our family survive? Would Poland survive?

Slowly the Eastern Front was collapsing; the German armies were falling back, the areas under their dominance contracting. The order had gone out from the German High Command that, where there was time, a scorched earth policy should be implemented in all areas they had to give up. Everything was to be destroyed.

The first two weeks of January were uneventful for us. Then shortly after midnight in the middle of the third week Szymon came banging on our front door. "Out, everybody out! The plant is on fire!" We jumped hurriedly in to our clothers and rushed outside.

One section of the plant was in flames. Two lines of drums, filled with lard and highly combustible were close to where the fire was raging and spreading alarmingly. My father shouted orders to Szymon, Maria and Hilary directing them to clear other combustibles well away from the flames and to fight the spread with water buckets and hoses.

My mother in panic called on me to go with her back to the house where we hurriedly dressed Waldemar and Joachim. I had an unspoken expectation that the German guards who would be checking the main road about this time must arrive at any time to get access to our phone and call the police and firefighting units. That, I was sure, was bound to expose all the illegal production my father was pursuing.

If the fire were to spread to other drums inside and outside in which lard for the soap manufacturing process was stored, then it would reach the coal store and everything would be incinerated.

Regulations required that every room in an industrial or manufacturing enterprise had to be stocked with firefighting equipment and utensils. We had all of these, buckets filled with sand, axes and spades and fire extinguishers. The plant had mostly tar and felt roofs, which burn quickly, but fortunately at this time of the year they were covered with 20 centimetres of snow.

After a while, since neither mother nor I could see any sign of the German guards coming, I wandered outside to see how the others were coping with the fire. I was amazed to see they had managed to get it somewhat under control. They were still working furiously, everyone covered in sweat and grime and I quickly joined them.

We worked on for several hours and there was still no sign of the German military or police, something we could not understand. Those patrolling the main road must surely have seen the flames.

The fire by now was well controlled and subdued but still smouldering in several areas. Sand covered most of the remaining combustible material. Everyone traipsed into the house totally exhausted.

My father was the most exhausted of all. My mother made tea for us. We sat around the table and reflected on how our small household had managed to get such a fierce fire under control.

And why had the Germans not arrived? It was all so hard to believe. But my father at least had his own explanation and conviction. To him it was the hand of providence. "So long as we fight on," he said, "we shall survive this war. God will see to it."

Next morning our workers arrived and set about cleaning up and removing all traces of the fire.

We were having breakfast a couple of weeks later when three most unwelcome people arrived at our door, a policeman, a fire officer and a Nazi Party official. They advised they had come for a fire safety inspection. It had nothing to do with the fire we had just had but the German authorities were very strict on fire safety precautions, so this visit was hardly a surprise although it was a first for us.

My father immediately got up from the table and motioned to take them out to the plant.

He simply couldn't afford to have an inspection of the house, particularly the garret where all our contraband production was stored. Indeed he was overanxious, aware that there was a strong smell in the passageway where they were standing from the lard, pork fat and smoked meat above.

If he could get these three out to the plant, then it might give the rest of us an opportunity to take the stuff from the garret and hide it.

"No, no," the Nazi official insisted. "Go inside and have your breakfast. We'll inspect the house first." He motioned the fire officer to the stairway to the garret. My father tried inviting them into the living room for a coffee but no they had their work to do. He pushed my father into the living room and closed the door after him.

Inside my mother at the table had turned pale, a dreadful expression on her face. Now she began to shake uncontrollably. In the garret, we all knew, was evidence to destroy the whole family. My father put a comforting hand on her shoulder to steady her, and Hilary and I was stunned at the seizure of fear that had gripped her. We heard footsteps ascending the stairs to the garret.

We didn't dare dwell on what was about to happen. Then we heard a voice from the garret calling to somebody below: *"Hier ist alles in Ordnung."* We could not believe it. Everything is in order. Was the man blind? Had he no sense of smell? Even on the stairs that smell of freshly smoked ham was evident. We looked at each other. Mother's face sagged visibly. The Nazi official opened the door and beckoned my father. "Come now," he said, "let's go over to the factory."

Mother was breathing freely again but she never left the table until my father returned and told us the German officials had left. Then she got to her feet and clasped my father in her arms. She could hardly believe we had survived but my father assured her that everything was fine.

"But for how long?" she asked him. "For how long?"

He looked at her, his eyes troubled. He knew how mentally exhausted she was, but he also knew there was no other way for them; they had to help the suffering people around them.

She pleaded with him. "Can't you see how fatigued I am? And the children, it is so hard on them. How much longer do you expect us to keep going? Day after day, night after night, for more than four years now, under constant pressure, never knowing when the final hour will come, when we may be sent to our deaths. Don't you realise we cannot go on forever getting away with all this? This morning we are lucky again, but what about next time? Tonight? Tomorrow? And there is no way of telling how long the war will last."

Calmly my father guided her back to her chair and sat down himself again with us. I was conscious now that I was going to be late for school but I also knew that my German teacher, the *'Wanze'*, had of late become increasingly indifferent as to whether we attended or not. And it was more important for me to stay here now and listen while my parents resolved this awful dilemma.

I could sense that my father wanted to explain something to us but was having difficulty expressing himself. We had all become quiet with expectation and finally he spoke.

"Children, we should all be proud of Mum doing so much for people with so little to look forward to except fear and hunger and death. While we still go to bed fed and warm, there are hundreds of thousands of others who go cold, sick and hungry. We cannot be indifferent to this. And without Mum's continuing efforts and courage we could not go on helping others. We could not fulfil the promise I have made to God many times that if he protected us we would go on helping and saving others. Now we cannot escape this. We cannot stop doing what we are doing, no matter how great the risk, especially now. Maybe within another year this terrible war will come to an end, then we can all be happy again and thank God for protecting us."

We absorbed all he said. It would never have occurred to us to dispute a word. I was soon on my way to school.

C·H·A·P·T·E·R 16

Despair Growing – The Decline of the Reich

BETWEEN THE END of November 1943 and mid June 1944 news continued to filter through to us that brought much optimism to our family and the depressed people around us. First, that Churchill, Roosevelt and Stalin had met at Teheran; then, later, that the Allies had landed at Anzio in Italy and that the long siege of Leningrad had ended.

The next particularly significant news gave rise to much euphoria. The Polish Army had captured Monte Casino and opened the way to Rome. We learned of the opening of the second front with the Allies landing at Normandy in France and that the Soviets had captured Brest-Litovsk on their way to Warsaw.

Now one question began to dominate the minds of all Poles: who would be the first to arrive to liberate Poland? Would it be the Polish Army coming from the north of Rome, the Allies from the West or the Soviets from the East?

Whenever my father could find time he would spend it with us in the evenings, usually around the bench in the garden. Here I would prime him with questions trying to ascertain his views as to who would arrive first in to Poland. He was to all of us a fundamental source of knowledge and we had absolute faith in him. But the views he expressed were sobering.

"Ted," he told me one evening when I had him on his own, "we Poles have learned some hard lessons in our one thousand years of history. Polish generals, like Kosciuszko and Pulaski, fought for American freedom in the War of Independence. Polish pilots have been defending Britain against the German Luftwaffe. But who defended us against Germany in September 1939? We were betrayed by the Western Allies and attacked by the Soviets from the east. And who knows, maybe now in Teheran that sad history will be repeated. It would not surprise me if Churchill and Roosevelt sold out Poland to Stalin who will try to make this country another Soviet republic."

"Hitler's national-socialism and Stalin's communism have a lot in common. They both want to destroy Christianity, especially in Poland. They both have a social system in which all economic activity is conducted by the state dominated by a self-perpetuating totalitarian party."

He had to explain to me what 'self-perpetuating' meant, then went on: "In the past 25 years the Soviet regime has twice determined to take over Poland. Now, I greatly fear it will happen with the acquiescence of America. That means our freedom will be sacrificed again. Maybe lost forever."

"Do you remember, Ted, what I told you what Hitler once said about Poland?"

Yes, I remembered and repeated it to him. "That as long as he failed to destroy the Polish people's faith in God, so long he would fail to get dominance over them."

My father nodded and continued.

"And that is what has happened. And if the Soviets take over Poland, sooner or later they will face the same problem and will have as little success."

"We can be glad with all our hearts that the war will soon end but we cannot look forward to any joy in the foreseeable future. Believe me, Ted, we are a small nation of 30 million people. We don't have the military strength to match the more powerful nations around us. But we have one greater strength, our faith in God, and with this we have proven many times we can defeat more powerful nations."

Out of all of this I was confused, not knowing what to expect from the future. I hoped he was wrong in his assessment of the great powers in their attitude to Poland but I knew he wouldn't say what he did if he was not deeply convinced about it.

Every so often when I went with either of my parents to Szamotuly we would stop in Galowo and deliver a parcel to a woman whose husband had been taken away by the Germans. I was usually required to stay outside the house and look out for anybody approaching.

On one occasion my mother told me to come into the small room where the lady lived. After several minutes of conversation with my mother the lady shifted a cupboard and from behind it a pale thin middle aged man came out. I knew instinctively he was a Jew and wondered how he could fit behind the cupboard until the lady showed me how they had removed bricks from the old thick wall behind to make a space for him. He had been hiding there for more than two years since he had escaped from a train transporting him to the Warsaw ghetto.

I understood now why my parents would stop there and in the future, I was told, it was I who would deliver the parcels to the house.

In the second half of 1944 we could see that the Germans were becoming indifferent in their observation and regimentation of the Poles. Their vacant depressed expressions showed that they realised the war, for most of them, was lost. The day and night bombardments of Germany were having a dreadful effect. Despair was growing.

The Germans were also desperate for labour. Children and adults were rounded up in many places in Poland and sent to forced labour in Germany.

On one occasion I was with my father in Poznan. It was a warm summer's day and we were walking in the city centre. Suddenly from all directions huge trucks arrived with soldiers and police who checked the identities of all on the streets. The Poles, we could see, were being singled out and forced into the trucks. My father on impulse told me to come quickly and we ran into a narrow passageway which led into a yard. We found a small shed heaped with rubbish bins and hid for about an hour until we were sure the raid was over.

This time we were lucky but I was not so lucky a few days later when I was carrying parcels on my bike to Szamotuly post office. I had to leave my bike against a wall while I delivered the parcels to the right person. When I returned my bike was gone. In its place, stuck on the wall, was a notice with a stamp and signature. It read: *"Rader musen rollen fur den Sieg."* Yes indeed. Wheels must rotate for victory.

I was furious. This had finally happened to me and I could do nothing about it. There was no chance my father could get me another bike.

I began to search my brain for ideas to speed up the defeat of the Germans. I worked out a plan and took my best friend Wladek Kaczmarek into my confidence. I could not tell my parents but knew I could trust Wladek absolutely. And anyway I needed him to help me. My plan was to confuse the German military moving north, west and south by switching the signposts on the main roads, especially at intersections. Wladek was full of enthusiasm and we went to work, one of us on look-out while the other did the switching. We could then watch from a distance to see what effect we had. It didn't work all the time but sufficiently often to satisfy us.

In late summer and early autumn all available Poles were called up to dig trenches along the main routes. There were mainly two types of trenches: wide trenches to inhibit enemy tanks, narrow trenches to facilitate defending infantry. On the weekends my father, Hilary and I were involved in digging a short trench on the main road between Szamotuly and Lipnica. My father, to our amusement, likened this to digging German graves. It was, in a way, prophetic. These short rectangular trenches were intended to help refugees on the roads escape from the Soviet aircraft. Later on the advancing infantry and motorised units used them to dump the corpses of the fleeing Germans

The atmosphere on these digging projects was relaxed, almost high spirited. Everybody spoke Polish and the German guards no longer cared. Many of them were now anxious to ingratiate themselves with us. The situation had changed and was changing more every day. Everything was different for us now. Every day we could see new evidence of the decline of the German Reich.

In mid–November the first frosty weather arrived and was quickly followed by snow. Every week the weather grew harsher. We had had three mild winters. Now we were expecting a bitter one.

The main road, less than 200 metres from our property, was packed day and night with Germans, soldiers and civilians, making their way back to the Reich. Some were a sorry sight. For the first time in my life I saw part frozen people without noses or ears, suffering bedraggled soldiers returning from the eastern front. Some were scarcely 15 years old. A few when they came by our house would come in to warm themselves and my mother, sorry for them, especially the boys, would make them a warm drink, reflecting on how blindly they had followed Hitler. Sometimes they would ask for a place to hide but we advised them against that because at night the partisans came looking for Germans and in the day the SS were at large looking for partisans and deserters.

I thought back on a few months earlier when I had read one day in the newspaper the *Gauleiter* of the Poznan region, Arthur Greiser, had announced from Poznan Town Hall that: *"So lange der Himmel über der Erde ist, so lange bleibt das Reichsgau Warthegau Deutsch!"*

I could still see the sky above the earth but I knew it wasn't going to remain German for very long.

The German school I had been forced to attend was already abandoned, the *'Wanze'* one of the first to flee.

Almost every day now I would spend several hours on the road, often in temperatures around minus 30 degrees, watching the German refugees fleeing. I recalled that the weather had been much kinder in those seemingly distant days of September 1939 when the defenceless Polish people were fleeing eastwards in overloaded carts and wagons and the advancing German military were firing on them indiscriminately. Now the fierce icy winds were killing the children and the elderly huddled in their carts and wagons as the pathetic German refugees fled westwards to their devastated homeland.

I could hear the crying of the children and women as the refugee columns continued for weeks, interspersed with retreating military columns.

175

One night during the first week of the New Year 1945 while we were all sleeping we were wakened by persistent knocking on the shutter of the bedroom window at the forest side of the house. As my father climbed from his bed, telling to us to keep quiet, the knocking came again and a voice whispering urgently: "Czeslaw... Klara..."

My father recognised the voice. It was Stanislaw Sobiszewski, his brother-in-law from Inowroclaw. He was a locomotive manager and had abandoned his train, taking refugees back to Germany, when it was forced to halt during the night.

Soon we were all up listening to his story with interest and learning from him what was happening in other parts of Poland. Then my father showed him a secure place to hide until it was safe for him to return home.

A few days later, at eight in the evening, we received a phone call from the authorities instructing us to go immediately to Brodziszewo and advise the *Reichsarbeitsdienstmädchen* (Girls farm and land army) that they must vacate their barracks by midnight. My father sent Szymon to do this.

Shortly after midnight we could hear them taking a short cut through the forest past our house, pushing bikes and carts loaded with all they could take. We could hear every step the unhappy contingent made in the frozen snow and it brought home to us again how time for the German was fast running out.

The next day we received a visit from some high ranking German officials. They did not come in but spoke with my father outside, then went with him to the garage where the Citroën truck was kept. Some 15 minutes later they left.

When he came in my father told us he had been informed that his truck would be the last to leave Szamotuly and would carry the last official documents out of Poznan province together with 15 top officials of the Reich. He had to have the truck ready and wait for their call.

All the family realised that this could spell the end for our father as well. Mother was very distressed. She berated my father for putting so much effort into keeping the truck mobile.

"Don't give up yet," my father told her. "This is not the end. Now please get me ready for tomorrow a small suitcase with food." He then put on his overcoat and went out. I could sense they wanted to avoid any further discussion or recrimination.

He returned a few hours later and sat with us for the midday meal. Immediately after the meal he instructed us that if any call came from the German authorities we should say he was in the garage repairing the truck. He explained that electric wires under the truck had short-circuited and he would try to repair it. At this my mother got very upset and her voice showed it.

"You know the Germans will see this as sabotage and will execute you on the spot. Have no doubt about it. Better we should escape from here now and hide for a few days until we know the Germans have gone."

My father would have none of this. He shook his head. "We cannot run away, especially now. We have to look after this place as long as we can. We must trust in God's providence. He has never let us down and won't now, when maybe hundreds will be starving and we must help them. I have to keep the truck here because there won't be any other truck or means of transport available."

From this moment the situation in our household became very tense. Mother was again in a very nervous state, concerned for all of us.

Hilary was indifferent. He had said to me long before that when the day came he would join the partisans in the forest. I considered the situation from all angles. I thought about mother, Dad and Hilary. I questioned myself again and again and in the end decided I would stay by my father's side. He was the one that had taught me to be strong, that good would always triumph over bad. He had proven it to me many times over the past terrible five years. "If you believe in God, he will not fail you." I had heard it from him so many times and I believed him. Nothing bad was going to happen to us now.

We both tried to reassure mother but every time the phone rang she went into a state bordering on panic. And the phone seemed to ring more frequently than ever. Friends were trying to ensure we were all right and would inform us of what was happening around the district.

The heavy bombardment was now a daily routine and then we began to hear the sound of the heavy artillery, at first far away but growing closer with every passing hour. The battle for Poznan had begun. The last news we heard was that the Germans, in retreat, were burning down house after house, destroying street after street and that the Soviet Army was trying to encircle them.

The Poles who had been phoning us and those near us were dreading now that the Soviets might repeat here what they had done at Warsaw when they halted at the other side of the river Vistula and let the Germans slaughter the defenceless Polish population. Would they stop at the river Warta now and leave us at the mercy of the Germans.

My father that evening said the next two days would determine whether we would stay here or go. We were all awake beyond midnight, conscious that it could be our last night together. We knelt for the family rosary and then went to bed while my father continued with his prayers. Later he came to bed but only partly undressed in case the Germans might arrive during the night.

Next morning he went out to the garage where the Citroën truck was. There was little activity at the plant, which was now putting in less than one shift a day. The Germans no longer concerned themselves about production.

Inside the house the first phone call came. Mother picked up the receiver. It was a friend telling us that last night a Soviet detachment had killed all the German *'Volkssturm'* (latterly conscripted old men) assembled in front of the party building and there were now no Germans on the streets.

Mother was relieved, convinced that all the Germans had left Szamotuly. We went out to the garage to tell father the news. Inside the house the phone rang again and I ran and picked it up. An authoritative voice told me to get my father to the phone. *"Ja, aber sofort!"* I rushed out to call my father and listened while he spoke on the phone. I could hear the loud voice at the other end. Within one hour he was to pick them up with the truck at Szamotuly. My father explained that he was trying to fix the electrical wiring and that it would take him longer. The voice at the other end began to yell so loud that my father held the receiver away from his ear. They gave him until six o'clock to be in Szamotuly. He said he would do his best and put down the phone.

My mother, now at his shoulder, had heard the end of the conversation.

"What are you going to do?" she asked.

"I'm going to keep the truck but I must play for time. They don't have much time until the Russians arrive in Szamotuly."

"Our lives depend on that truck," mother said. "Before the Russians get them, they'll get us."

A little later Hilary left for the forest, saying he would be back in a few days.

As the hands on the clock face moved towards 6 pm the tension in the house grew ominously. Just before six my father arrived in from the shed. A couple of minutes later the phone rang. My mother calmly picked it up. She told the caller my father was still under the truck but should be able to pick them up in an hour or two. The voice at the other end began to yell. "If that pig is not here very soon, we'll be there to get him."

We sat together in the room saying very little. My father obviously was not going back to the garage. I realised then he never had any intention of having the truck ready for the Germans.

A little over an hour later the phone rang again. This time it was a Polish voice, a man we did not know. He was phoning, he said, to warn us that three Germans in black overcoats (obviously SS) had just left in a small open vehicle for our place; that we should hide. Mother thanked him. His only words were: "We will pray for you. God bless you." He put down the phone.

There was little time left for us now. Father spoke quietly to each of us in turn, Joachim, Waldemar, me and mother, saying we should not be afraid, that nothing would happen to us.

He went to the door, stopped for a moment in front of the crucifix, then turned back towards us and made the Sign of the Cross. We each blessed ourselves. He took the little suitcase which mother had packed for him, draped his warm overcoat over his arm and went out to the garage.

I looked at mother's face. For once it was expressionless as if suspended in time. But I knew what she was thinking. Soon the Germans would arrive and none of us would survive when they could not pick up the truck.

We sat down on the couch and mother took Joachim on her knee. She seemed to have overcome the fear inside as she reminded us of the good times we had shared with our father. Sitting beside her in the warm room we felt sorry for him, outside in the cold garage, where the temperature was minus 30 degrees.

The heavy traffic on the main road had grown silent and now suddenly we could hear the noise of the car turning off the road towards our house. Minutes later a loud shout carried across the cold night.

"Aufmachen. Schnell!"

Szymon's voice answered, he would have to lock up the dogs, then he would open up. We heard them drive into the plant yard, yelling loudly in anger.

Mother stood up and began to shake. She tried to say something but couldn't. A minute or two passed, then a loud shot cracked the silence. Mother gasped "Oh God!" I began to shake, certain my father had been shot and soon all of as would die.

Mother clasped us around her and suddenly relaxed, almost indifferent. The seconds grew into minutes and the passing minutes seemed like hours and still they hadn't come for us. And now we could hear the engine start up and the vehicle was driving away very quickly. The tears were running down mother's cheeks; Joachim and Waldemar were crying. There were cold tears in my eyes but I could not cry, simply because I could not understand what was happening. Had God finally let my father down?

"No, it's not true!" I was shouting. "I don't believe God has let him down."

Mother was looking at me, alarmed, when suddenly the door opened and my father walked in slowly, the suitcase in his hand. I had the feeling mother was going to faint, then father rushed across and held her in his arms. I was suddenly relaxed and happy but I couldn't speak a word. I reached for my father's right hand and kissed it.

There was silence for a while, nobody wanting to speak, then mother recovered and asked father:

"What was the shot?"

"One of them fired a shot at me while I was under the truck but the other hit his arm as he pulled the trigger. 'Let the Polish pig live. We'll have time to finish him later.'"

"God works in strange ways. He was SS and had probably killed dozens of people. I couldn't see his face but something told me he didn't want to have me on his conscience."

"There's no time for them to come back. Time has run out for them and for the brutality they have inflicted on our people. Let us thank God."

"For us now the war is almost over. There was no break in the electric circuit. I put a flame to the wiring under the truck. I'm glad I did. I think we're going to need the truck now to bring help and supplies to our people."

Two days later, we learned, a group of 15 German officials had organised an old tractor with a trailer and a Polish driver to get out of Szamotuly. Early next morning they had just reached the forest near Wronki when the driver disappeared into the forest. Shortly afterwards they ran into a detachment of Soviet soldiers, who recognised them as SS and shot all of them.

C·H·A·P·T·E·R   17

The Russians Waste No Time

O N THE MORNING OF 25 JANUARY, 1945 a strange calm seemed to have settled on the snow-covered countryside. For the first time in a long while we began to feel that we were safe. Even mother was visibly relaxed and composed. At the same time, in the far distance, we could hear artillery fire, the crackle of rifles and the rattle of machine guns. This was loud at times and seemed excessive. The heavy snow falling kept us inside all day, then at four in the afternoon it stopped.

My father told me to put on some warm clothes; we were going outside. We went up to the plant to collect Szymon who was the only one left there. Since yesterday all the machinery had come to a halt.

He led us off towards the forest and I wondered why he was taking us there. Perhaps he sensed the Russians were coming and it was his habit in such circumstances to go out to meet anyone arriving.

We stood at the edge of the road and the forest and did not have to wait long. Suddenly out of the forest a figure in white emerged on a long sledge drawn by four white husky dogs. We waved and he came up to us, an elderly Russian soldier with a machine gun mounted on the sledge and a box of ammunition beside it. His first words to us were: "Are you Poles?"

"Yes", we answered in unison.

"And where are the Germans?" he asked.

My father explained that the last of the Germans had left Szamotuly that morning.

As we stood in discussion with this Russian soldier, the first I had met, I was surprised how easy it was to communicate with him. Finally, satisfied that we were not enemies, he urged the dogs around and disappeared back into the forest.

Half an hour later, on the road from Brodziszewo, a column of Russian tanks came by followed by a horse drawn cart filled with soldiers. We waved a welcome to them as they passed.

Back home an hour later we shared our impressions with mother and Marie. But Szymon was less impressed than we were by the first Russians, his countrymen that he had seen in a long time. "Boss", he told my father, "I don't think they have changed much. They are still the same rabble they were 25 years ago."

"Szymon," my father answered, "Russia still has the same system you left behind in 1920. Deep down these are good people but the Stalinist system has destroyed their humanity."

Surprisingly, our phone was still working, so my father used it to get in touch with some friends in Szamotuly to tell them the Russians were arriving. Because he knew of the Russian tactic to first encircle a town or city before entering it, he was not surprised to learn they had not arrived in Szamotuly.

A phone call from one of our friends next evening told us the Russians had at last arrived and had announced their arrival by firing the first shot into the big clock on Railway Street. There was no fighting because all the Germans had left. But there had been some resistance from German stragglers hiding in the forest.

We were lucky in that the Red Army had advanced quickly through our area, giving the Germans little opportunity to persue their normal policy of total destruction in retreat — executions, burning of houses and blowing up bridges. For us at last the war was over. After five terrible years we could relax — at least for the time being.

※

My father's first priority was to reverse the 'sabotage' work on his truck so that it would be ready for the road as soon as possible. His second priority was to organise people who would help him to get together the supplies left behind by the Germans — food, milk and flour — in their hurried retreat and who would help him in his efforts to distribute these supplies in Poznan. But first he had to learn the situation in Poznan, which was now in Russian hands.

Within three days the food supplies began arriving at our plant from around the countryside. The news had spread quickly that we had saved our truck and that it was the only one in the district still mobile.

Push carts and sledges began to arrive, loaded with whatever supplies could be found. The people knew my father could be relied upon to get these to starving people wherever they might be located.

Poznan, which had a Polish population of a quarter of a million, was the last bastion of Nazi resistance in Middle

West Poland. And the news had reached us that the notorious Nazi 'Brandkommando' had been let loose on the city burning down residential buildings, schools and hospitals.

My father wanted to waste no time in getting his relief project moving. On 28 January he was ready with four men. The Citroën truck was loaded to capacity with food, milk and soap. It moved out of our plant with two men armed with machine guns mounted on the mudguards on either side, another in the cabin with my father and a fourth with a rifle in the back. Knowing their mission was dangerous, my father made the Sign of the Cross as he said good-bye to us. The others, observing this, did the same.

As we went back into the house with my mother, she carried a worried expression. She knew his health was not good; he had been suffering with his kidneys for almost two years. She also knew the patched-up Citroën was not reliable and wondered how far it would carry them. They could loose everything and might be lucky to save their own lives. But she also knew nothing would stop my father carrying out what he had planned to do for a long time.

She also worried about Hilary and wondered if he was still alive. But she knew he was strong and that thought gave her strength too.

The truck had left about 10am in the direction of Szamotuly. Poznan was 45 kilometres away through several villages and forestland, and the journey should take about an hour each way.

A little later some Polish farm workers who had been working on German farms arrived with food supplies and milk. Then after we had finished our dinner, around 1pm, we heard the Citroën arriving back. Father invited his four helpers in for a meal and told Szymon and me to get to work loading the Citroën again. Shortly everyone came out again and helped to load.

My father did not say much, but concentrated on his work. He was clearly in his element, full of motivation. Some two hours later the truck moved off again and I went immediately to find out what I could from mother. She could only tell me that the Germans were still in the centre of Poznan and in the forest of Napachanie. They had opened fire on the truck as it was speeding through the forest.

Hostilities continued in and around the city of Poznan for a month, up to 23 February, 1945.

The Soviet Army engaged the 48,000 strong German garrison in fierce fighting but with no real intent to finish it off in the short term. As they had done elsewhere, in the furtherance of their calculated policy, they gave the Germans time and opportunity to destroy all they could and turn vast sections of the old city to ashes, especially those areas which were a reminder of Poland's past and culture.

When more than 40 per cent of the city had been destroyed the local inhabitants would wait no longer. They equipped themselves with what arms they could find and took on the Germans themselves. The bitterest fighting was around the citadel which continued as a fortress and bulwark for the German Army until, finally, after two days of immense losses, the Polish volunteers brought freedom to the exhausted city.

A few days later I asked my father if I could go with him to Poznan to see for myself what had happened. He was reluctant, explaining that it could be too dangerous but finally gave way to my insistence and agreed.

The truck was loaded mostly with containers of fresh milk. I sat in the cabin beside my father who told me, as we hurried along the uneven road, that I should continue talking to him to keep him awake as he had not had much sleep. All those helping with my father's supply run were sleeping only in short breaks.

It was morning when we arrived in the western outskirts of the city which was not greatly damaged. Ahead of us I could see a group of people coming towards us. They were weak and ragged, mainly women with children and a few old men. For three consecutive days they had been waiting for my father's truck which was trying to serve different locations.

There were expressions of joy when they recognised my father. Some women kissed his hand to thank him. But on the faces of the old people there was little sign of the hope the Soviet liberation was supposed to bring.

Hurriedly, my father, and the other men who had travelled with us, began distributing the milk to the crowd which was growing larger with each passing minute. Suddenly a Soviet military truck drove up and came to a halt in front of our vehicle. A Soviet officer alighted and, accompanied by a soldier, approached my father demanding to know what was going on. My father explained politely that he was distributing milk he had collected.

What! The officer frowned, then turned and issued a command to four soldiers sitting in the back of the truck to empty the rest of the milk containers on to the street. Angrily he bellowed to my father that this was contaminated German milk and if he saw our truck coming here again he would confiscate it.

My father tried to negotiate with him, observing the hungry people were distressed and growing agitated. To no avail. After the soldiers had poured all the milk on to the street the officer ordered them back on to the truck and drove quickly away, leaving the women in tears and the children crying.

My father had to summon all his patience and restrain himself. He realised that the man was a political officer with the power of life and death in his hands. He could find no way to explain the incident to the people who, for the first time, were getting a taste of Soviet "liberation".

Standing there, dismayed, they expressed their anger looking after the departing truck. "They have let millions of their own people starve to death," one man said. "Now they are trying the same on us."

Before he drove away my father arranged another place to rendezvous next time. As long as he could continue to get food supplies he was determined to go on making these trips to Poznan day and night.

The dilapidated old Citroën truck refused to falter. Day after day it kept running without giving any trouble. Also my father's health seemed to blossom in all this activity. But later he would bear the consequences. Meanwhile Hilary returned home after an absence of some three weeks and often replaced my father in the driving seat of the truck.

In Szamotuly the Soviets wasted no time. Quickly they set up their own commissariat under Major Grigorij Kuzmicz and Major Kazanow. These were instructed by the Soviet command to organise throughout the whole Szamotuly region civilian authority, local government and local militia, implementing systematic Soviet style control.

For eight consecutive weeks from the end of January, along the main roads, came columns of the Soviet Army interspersed with units of the Polish Army which had been mobilized in the Soviet Union. Day and night they moved non-stop in the direction of Berlin. Some of the heavy military trucks, supplied by the USA to the Soviets, still showed the big white star of the Americans, suggesting the Soviets hadn't had time to paint them over. Many times in the sky overhead heavily loaded bomber aircraft passed over our place.

But Hitler in his fanaticism was not yet ready to surrender. He continued to send out his paratroopers, many of whom landed in our region. Some put up resistance but many committed suicide. They were mostly young men, forced into SS Units, as if in the knowledge that the Soviets would execute them on the spot. Hitler had once declared to the nation that when he had to go down the 'Volk' would have to go with him! Throughout the month of February fighting still went on in our region.

In our home early one frosty morning we heard repeated revolver shots which awoke us. A strange silence followed with only the sound of the Soviet columns moving along the main road. We dressed and, after breakfast, I put on a warm coat and went to the forest. I found many footsteps in the snow and followed them. Shortly I came to a place where 10 young German SS lay dead, their bodies frozen. Each had put a revolver into his mouth and shot himself. I went straight home and called my parents.

My father called Szymon and told him to take a pick and spade and bury the corpses, but first take their ID documents. I went with Szymon to show him where they were lying which was close to the trenches we had dug some time before. Szymon buried them there, as the frozen ground was almost impossible to dig.

My mother collected all the ID cards along with others we had taken from bodies at different times. When the war was over she had about twenty in all and wrote to the families notifying them of the fate of their sons or husbands. Several were young married men but of some of the families there was no trace, so she sent the ID cards to the German Red Cross.

Other families asked for the documents and, if possible, photographs of the graves or a description of where their sons and husbands lay. They were grateful for what my mother had done and, even several years later, we were receiving parcels as a sign of their gratitude.

C·H·A·P·T·E·R 18

The Reign of the Devil

THE WAR WAS NOT YET OVER when news reached us of the agreement signed at Yalta on 12 February by Roosevelt, Churchill and Stalin giving control of Poland to the Soviet Union and ensuring that it would be the Red Army and not the armies of the western allies that reached Berlin on 20 April. This brought dismay and fear to the great mass of the Polish people.

My father was consumed by sadness. What he had assumed would happen at Teheran was now finally confirmed at Yalta: there would be no free Poland.

When he received an order to hang out on May Day the red and white national flag of Poland he refused. May Day was the big national holiday of the Soviet Union not of Poland. Poland's holiday had been Constitution Day, 3 May, but that date was to be ignored by the new communist government.

"This is not for us," he told the family, shaking his head, "the free Poland for which millions have given their lives."

The German unconditional surrender came on 7 May. The end of World War 2 in Europe was celebrated on 9 May around the world. But for Poland, in my father's words, this was the beginning of "the reign of the devil".

"The Soviets," he told us, "will try to introduce their system of communism to Poland, a system of social organization in which all economic activity is conducted by a totalitarian state dominated by a single self-perpetuating political party."

"They will conspire clandestinely to further their evil purpose. They will try to take our possessions and property, to destroy all private industry like ours and impose their monuments and relics. Ultimately they will try to put an end to our belief in the Christian faith."

His next words were directed to me personally and I have never forgotten them. "Ted, believe me and remember what I am telling you. My health is not the best and I am not likely to last too long after these hard times, but in 50 years from now, which you will see, you will witness the fall of this communist regime. I believe that our nation's strong Christian foundation will, sooner or later, conquer this communist system."

My father's self-imposed mission to help others survive the war was now at an end. Time and again we have heard him affirm that "only with God's help can we survive". And we were well aware that only his strong faith and trust in God had enabled us to survive in the forest. Ours was the only factory in the whole of occupied Poland to remain in Polish hands.

It was a source of great sadness to my parents that there was no trace of the brave, Dr. Von Der Ouwe or of any of the Hermesmann family.

My elder brother Hilary, my close friend Wladek and I had returned to school on 19 February 1945. On 1 September that year my younger brother Waldemar started school in Brodziszewo.

My father was looking forward to renovating the plant so that production could start again as soon as possible. He had decided that the first soap production in Poland after the war would carry the brand names *'Czeka'* and *'Teka'*, which were his and my Christian names.

At the beginning of winter 1946 my father was instructed by the Government authorities to process more than 80 train loads of raw salt herrings into herring oil. As our factory equipment was ideal for this process he was happy to accept the order.

Thousands of these barrels of herrings had been donated shortly after the war by the USA to the hungry people of Poland. However the Soviets and the Soviet installed Polish Government refused to distribute them, anxious that the people should not know the extent to which the USA was helping. Instead they left the barrels for many months lying in the open air until the contents were spoiled. After this they were sent to my father for processing into oil.

By 1947 my father's Citroën truck was worn out and he was searching for a replacement but couldn't find anything. Finally in the autumn of 1948 he managed to buy a 3.5-ton Klockner Deutz truck, which had been assembled from miscellaneous parts.

But then just as everything was running well he was confronted by more and more difficulties orchestrated by the communist authorities. They tried to bend him financially but he defied them and met all his financial obligations.

The pressure was taking its toll however and suddenly he became gravely ill. Since 1944 he had been suffering kidney disease and now had to face an operation. He was given only a small chance to survive but the operation went well and survive he did after the removal of 23 kidney stones. In three weeks he returned home.

As soon as he recovered he started to expand our house and erect a temporary storage building. After 20 years in the forest, going through the hardest of times, first the Great Depression and then the war, everything was finally beginning to turn in his favour. Then came the final blow.

One sunny morning, totally unexpected, a party of five government officials arrived at our property and declared it was being commandeered and would now become government property.

This announcement shocked my parents. My father declined to accept the post of manager which they offered him and was then given official notice in writing that the property and its contents had to be abandoned within a few days. He was allowed to keep the two trucks and what possessions and furniture he could load on to them.

He was advised that a (communist) party member would now be appointed to run the place, a person whom he knew did not have the faintest knowledge of our machinery or processes and was incapable of running this kind of business.

My father refused them any co-operation and refused to leave. The stalemate continued for a month and, with my father still refusing to move, the authorities sent in workmen to demolish the roof of the house. The ceiling remained intact during some dry days that followed but as soon as it rained the water came through, running down the walls and soaking the wallpaper and carpets.

The mental effect on my mother was devastating. She could no longer handle these conditions. After another month of this my father realised our situation was hopeless.

He had a vacant block of land in Szamotuly which he had bought some years earlier and now decided he would try and build a house on this block. Since no new bricks were available for private construction the little house had to be built with second-hand bricks.

During this period my parents, forced to share one room during the day with the newly installed manager and his secretary, witnessed the gradual disintegration of the plant which represented much of his life's work.

For a while part production at the plant was maintained but by late August production had ceased completely. In a short while the rusting machinery was dismantled and removed and the home-in-the-forest of which we were once so proud became a devastated ruin.

This was the new planned socialist economy imposed on us by the Soviet Union.

We move into our new little house in Szamotuly and my father was reduced to earning a living by transport work using his dilapidated trucks.

In September 1947 I went to live in Poznan to attend business college and finished there in June 1951. In August that year I was called up for two years compulsory national service in the Polish Army. In the winter of 1952-53 I arrived home on short leave from the army and was dismayed to find my father was not there. My mother, anxious not to cause me concern, explained that the Security Police had taken him away a week earlier. For a long time he had stubbornly resisted their attempts to give false testimony against people he knew.

I was furious and straight away went down to the 'UB' (Security Police) building in my uniform and demanded to see my father. I had to wait more than an hour before my father was brought; we were then escorted to a room where they could hear our conversation. We were told we could have ten minutes together.

My father was pale and looked distressed. It was obvious he was going through a hard time. He had a cold and seemed worn out. We clasped each other and he whispered not to ask him questions but to listen. It must have been obvious to him that I was nervous. He asked me how I liked the army then answered himself saying that I must like the uniform. He asked about Mum, Hilary, Waldemar and Joachim. Then he wished me success and reminded me to pray that we might all be together again soon.

After we parted I didn't feel like going home. Instead I went to the church where I felt relaxed and glad to be alone with God. I was looking for answers. Why had this happened to my father? Tears filled my eyes and I reflected on what he had once said about "the reign of the devil". That's what it must be.

I wondered in what conditions he was being held. Perhaps he too was now standing in a dark cold cellar with the concrete floor covered in water. That's how I had been kept last Christmas just because they had caught me singing carols which was prohibited in the army.

Would I, in this awful system, share the same fate as my parents? Throughout the war they had constantly risked their lives to save others. They had survived to see the end of hostilities: then they had lost everything. And now my father was locked away because he had refused to bear false witness against innocent people.

I felt helpless. I could do nothing except pray for my father and trust in God that he would soon be released.

As I left the church the same question pervaded my thought. Must I too go through all this? Was there no way out for me? I was, after all, the only one in my family with a penchant for wandering and travelling. Suddenly I was conscious of a gleam of hope.

Why not get away from under this communist regime and make my way somewhere to a country that was free? But, being a Pole incarcerated in Poland, there was little choice for me. Poland was surrounded by communist neighbours: in the East the Soviet Union, in the South Czechoslovakia, West the German Democratic Republic and to the North the cold Baltic Sea. To leave my country legally was beyond my power.

And what would happen to my parents if I managed to leave Poland illegally? I would expose them to great danger from the Office of Security.

But the thought persisted and I found myself planning for a future believing that one day the chance would come. Any attempt to desert from the army was out of the question. If I failed it would be tantamount to a death sentence. I had to avoid decisions that spelled only disaster.

While I could see no future I could not avoid preparing myself for a day when I would leave my beloved country.

Three days after returning to barracks I phoned home and was overjoyed to find myself speaking to my father. Earlier that day he had been released. We did not speak for long aware that the Security Police might be listening in on our conversation. My father was so grateful that I had come to see him. This made me wonder. I was in fact the only person that had been allowed to visit him. Maybe the fact that I was in uniform had achieved the impossible. Maybe that was God's way of answering my prayer.

E·P·I·L·O·G·U·E

The Light at the End of the Tunnel

U P TO THE DEATH OF STALIN on 5 March, 1953 thousands in Poland were arrested, tortured or disappeared. It was
an absolute reign of terror, which improved a little after Stalin,
but the grim reality of the communist doctrine remained the
same.

On 28 June, 1956 the workers of Poznan had had enough
and rioted against the regime. After four days and with more
than 80 dead I personally witnessed the brutal crushing of
this uprising by the Red Army.

This first bloody protest in Poland resulted in a change of
Government but not of the system. It gave me a little
optimism that I might eventually escape. Some time later I
managed to bribe a high-ranking officer to obtain for me a
visa to the DDR (East Germany) for a short visit to the
Leipzig Fair.

At this time I was managing a state-owned department
store in Szamotuly and had little difficulty in finding a
replacement for two weeks. Towards the end of May 1957

I found myself crossing the Polish-German border. It took no more than a week in East Germany for me to observe that the communist system there was no better than in Poland, so I made my way to East Berlin where I managed to cross illegally into West Berlin. The wall had not yet been erected.

It is hard to describe my emotions standing for the first time in 'free' territory. But I was worried for my family who was sure to face some retribution. In fact the UB (Security Police) gave my parents no peace. Twice each week over the next eight weeks my parents were called to the UB headquarters where they were tortuously questioned and pressured to make me come back home.

Aware of what my parents were going through I decided to act. I put together a detailed letter of 12 pages, telling all of what my parents had done during the war, helping all those around them, and what ingratitude they were shown by the authorities after the war with their home and all their possessions taken from them. I explained that the same was not going to happen to me, that I would not live under such a system.

The original I sent under registered cover to the Security Office (UB) and a copy to my parents. It had the effect I wanted. My parents were never questioned again.

Until 1963 my parents continued to make a difficult living from transport but as the owners of a private company they were not entitled to any social or medical benefits or even an old age pension. To survive economically they were forced to sell the Klockner truck and later the little house in Szamotuly, buying instead a small unit in Poznan.

At the age of 65, so that he could qualify for some age pension, instead of retiring my father was forced to start work again as a caretaker and telephone operator in a government firm. Only after 10 years did this entitle him to hospital and medical care and a minimum age pension!

After some three months in West Berlin I went to settle in the south of West Germany. Without work for many months I had time to reflect on my life and evaluate my future. My wish was to get married and to leave Europe forever. It seemed to me that Europe and particular Poland, because of its geographical location, would always be troubled in the conflict between East and West.

In 1960 I married my Polish wife Halina and shortly afterwards we decided that our ultimate destination should be Australia which was as far away from Europe as we could get. Australia, we knew, had never in its 170 years of settlement by the white man experienced war on its own soil or what it meant to live in a totalitarian state.

We have never regretted that decision and in later years from Australia we have revisited our native Poland four times, twice during the communist regime and twice since it became a free democracy.

During the first and second visits plain clothes policemen were always shadowing us, monitoring our movements, but when we arrived on our third visit, on 8 November 1989, in Poznan we heard an official TV announcement informing us that "today, after 50 years, Poland is a free country again".

Eleven years earlier, on 16 October, 1978, Cardinal Karol Wojtyla became the first non-Italian in 400 years to be elected to the papacy, and the first Pole ever to hold that office. For me this was a sensational event and it occurred to me then that this might mark the beginning of the end for communist regimes everywhere.

It is a matter of history now that in September 1980 for the first time in a communist country a free independent Trade Union 'Solidarity', was born and within a short time had ten million members led by a young charismatic electrician, Lech Walesa. Solidarity shook not only Poland and its leadership but also the rulers of the Soviet Union and other communist countries. Conscious of the faith of ninety per cent of the Polish Catholic population I was reminded again of the words of my father to me in May 1945.

"Our strength is our faith in God and with this we are capable of defeating the most powerful tyrants."

In times of reflection I can still hear the tragic people as they were being forcibly evacuated by the Germans from the village of Brodiszewo. Beaten with batons but uncovered as they were forced on to trucks their voices had swollen with confidence. Loud enough to be heard kilometres away they sang traditional Polish hymns, 'God protect Poland' *(Boze cos Polske)* and 'Poland has not perished' *(Jeszcze Polska nie zginela)*, the Polish national anthem.

The powerful Soviet Union, too, had tried to keep Poland crushed under its heel but, as Stalin was once forced to concede, "Fitting communism to Poland is like fitting a saddle to a cow." The realities of postwar Poland reflected this.

My father's prayers had been answered. Years before he had seen the light at the end of the tunnel but he had not lived long enough to arrive there. Four and a half years earlier, and four months after the death of my mother, he was laid to rest.

Without my father's guidance and inspiration I would not have been able to survive this story much less write it. Having learned the lesson of experience, and been touched by his vision and faith in a better future, like him I too am convinced that, if we have faith, then nothing will fail.

THE END.

ORDER FORM

(Please print clearly)

Please send me .... copies of
...Then Nothing Will Fail *by Ted Kazmierski.*

NAME Mr/Mrs/Miss/Ms . . . .

. . . .

ADDRESS . . . .

. . . .

STATE. . . . . POSTCODE . . . .

Signature . . . .

Books can also be ordered by calling

07 5491 4968 or 041 478 8126 (mobile)

Please send cheque or money order ($19.95 plus $4.55 postage)

ORDER FORM

(Please print clearly)

Please send me .... copies of
...Then Nothing Will Fail *by Ted Kazmierski.*

NAME Mr/Mrs/Miss/Ms . . . .

. . . .

ADDRESS . . . .

. . . .

STATE. . . . . POSTCODE . . . .

Signature . . . .

Books can also be ordered by calling

07 5491 4968 or 041 478 8126 (mobile)

Please send cheque or money order ($19.95 plus $4.55 postage)

TED KAZMIERSKI

38 Allonga Street
Currimundi
Qld
4551

TED KAZMIERSKI

38 Allonga Street
Currimundi
Qld
4551